Right Here, Right Now

Life Stories from America's Death Row

Edited by **Lynden Harris**

WITH A FOREWORD BY **HENDERSON HILL**
& AN AFTERWORD BY **TIMOTHY B. TYSON**

DUKE UNIVERSITY PRESS DURHAM AND LONDON 2021

© 2021 Duke University Press
All rights reserved
Printed in the United States of America
on acid-free paper ∞
Designed by Aimee C. Harrison
Typeset in Portrait Text and Trade Gothic LT Std by
Westchester Publishing Services

LIBRARY OF CONGRESS CATALOGING-IN-PUBLICATION DATA
Names: Harris, Lynden, [date] editor. | Hill, Henderson,
writer of foreword. | Tyson, Timothy B., writer of afterword.
Title: Right here, right now : life stories from America's
death row / edited by Lynden Harris ; with a foreword by
Henderson Hill and an afterword by Timothy B. Tyson.
Description: Durham : Duke University Press, 2021.
Identifiers: LCCN 2020040893 (print)
LCCN 2020040894 (ebook)
ISBN 9781478011972 (hardcover)
ISBN 9781478014119 (paperback)
ISBN 9781478021421 (ebook)
Subjects: LCSH: Death row inmates—United States—
Biography. | Marginality, Social—United States—
Psychological aspects.
Classification: LCC HV8699.U5 R54 2021 (print) | LCC
HV8699.U5 (ebook) | DDC 365/.6092273—dc23
LC record available at https://lccn.loc.gov/2020040893
LC ebook record available at https://lccn.loc.
gov/2020040894

Cover art: Cerron Hooks, *Consider the Source*, from
Hidden Voices' *Serving Life* exhibit.

This book is dedicated to you, the readers and changemakers, by those living on America's Death Row:

"We're all strong men here, but to not have your suffering recognized is the greatest indignity to the human spirit. Thank you for breathing life into our weary, wounded souls."

Contents

Foreword

HENDERSON HILL

More than 2.3 million Americans are incarcerated across the nation for crimes great and small. How is it that a nation that trumpets its traditions of freedom and liberty vies for the international title of the largest carceral state? How is it that a disproportionate number of those prisoners are descendants of enslaved peoples and other people of color, the vast majority poor, and too many mentally ill?

Right Here, Right Now allows us to read the stories and hear the voices of men society has determined to be disposable, persons whose humanity is officially denied, prisoners who await the capricious call of the lottery-like summons to the execution chamber. There is a spiritual jubilee in the reading of *Right Here, Right Now*. Yes, reader, prepare to be liberated: freed from the fiction that these deplorables, condemned to death, are monsters, so very different from you and me that the only right response is to exterminate them. The stories compiled, and the voices amplified, in effect restore the 2,500 men and women on death row to the human family. Anonymous no more, monstrous ciphers never again. Read the vignette "Downpour" (chapter 5) and never look at an umbrella or experience a heavy rain without being reminded of moments of traumatic insecurity, or perhaps being moved by a warm remembrance of the nurture and protection of a loving caregiver.

Bryan Stevenson, founder of the Equal Justice Initiative, author of *Just Mercy: A Story of Justice and Redemption*, and visionary instituter of the Legacy

Museum: From Enslavement to Mass Incarceration and the National Memorial for Peace and Justice, has explained how it is that he could grow so close to and love each and every one of his clients, all of whom could be described as deeply impaired and broken, many under sentence of death. In *Just Mercy* Stevenson writes, "You can't effectively fight abusive power, poverty, inequality, illness, oppression, or injustice and not be broken by it. We are all broken by something. We have all hurt someone and have been hurt. We all share the condition of brokenness even if our brokenness is not equivalent. . . . [O]ur shared brokenness connected us."

For decades, I have been privileged to be part of a community of lawyers, advocates, investigators, volunteers, and experts who have come to know and love the men and women our courts have condemned to death. I am stronger, wiser, and more empathetic because of the intimacies shared in isolated cells, tear-stained letters, and hostile courtrooms. The great gift that *Right Here, Right Now* delivers to readers is a soul-stirring compilation of stories and shared intimacies that can be life changing. Will it be the brief "U-Turn" (chapter 15), or "Car Ride" (chapter 9), or perhaps "Better Off Dead" (chapter 22) that quickens in you the realization that these broken folks were hurt by lived experiences, some close to our own, some unimaginable. Who and what are the individuals, the institutions, the teachings, and the safe places that gave you and me opportunities to repair from similar insults? The natural follow-up: what if one or more of those safety valves had been available to the then child-victim, now death row inmate?

Right Here, Right Now compels readers to examine their own experiences and make connections to innocence, damage, resilience, and hope. For me, I was transported back more than a decade, to a quiet and lonely jail cell. To a long embrace, followed by tears. First a welling at the corners and then the ducts giving way to the torrent. I was fifty, native of the Bronx, a Harvard-trained death penalty lawyer holding on to a trembling, bantamweight high school dropout. In my mind's eye I was embracing my younger brother or any one of the legions of African American young men, from my neighborhoods in the Bronx, Washington, DC, or Durham, North Carolina, who but for one social safety net provision or another might have been in that cell with me. This young man, whom I will call Ronald, shuffled between the Badlands of North Philadelphia and bucolic eastern North Carolina, was now drawing his first breaths as one condemned to die in prison—serving multiple life-without-parole sentences. A jury had just spared him from the death penalty. There was no celebration. Relief, yes. Earlier bravado declaring that death by needle was better than life in a box had yielded to urgings about the resilience of the human spirit and the potential for growth and development that could not be curbed by prison bars. Still, Ronald sat waiting to be shackled and carted off to what we both imagined to be something of an abyss. He was hurting, fearful, wracked with guilt and remorse for the unspeakable damage he had wrought. The explosion of violence, just a week after he turned eighteen, came when the young man was feeling isolated and emotionally abandoned, even as he spent his life shuttled between family members in the North Carolina countryside. Three years later, he braced to step into the abyss, a lifetime of incarceration. Tragically, his nightmare resulted in all-too-real devastation for the community, leaving five bodies lifeless, felled by a gun that he held. As we separated, the painful truth that he would have to make this journey by himself was dawning on him; for almost two years, he had been supported by a committed defense team of skilled and caring lawyers, sensitive and empathetic investigators and mitigation specialists, brilliant expert witnesses. He would now be alone, the decompression cruel. After two years of devastating review of forensic files, extraordinary bonding, intimate sharing, we realized that when I left the cell, we would likely not see each other ever again. The cell door closed, I walked away, I cried, and I moved on. Next.

I have not seen Ronald since our goodbyes in the jail cell almost fifteen years ago. Reading the stories in *Right Here, Right Now*, a dozen or more of them so resonate with young Ronald's life, they could have been written by my former client. I have spoken with Ronald by phone, and we have corresponded by mail over the years; he speaks and writes like a graduate student. He so impressed as well-read, curious, sensitive, and socially engaged. Having avoided a death sentence, he was able not to hear the parting words North Carolina judges repeat by rote to the condemned: "May God have mercy on your soul." *Right Here, Right Now* brings forward the voices of prisoners who received that judicial benediction, even as they struggle to maintain connection to society and sustain the flicker of humanity that incarceration and its daily insults attempt to extinguish.

Right Here, Right Now makes an especially timely and important contribution to the current national discourse on criminal justice reform and the death penalty. Support for the death penalty has reached record lows, and skepticism about the penalty, a relic of the nation's history of slavery and racialized violence, is finding renewed purchase among religious and political conservatives. The national organization Conservatives Concerned about the Death Penalty supported the Republican-led campaign to repeal the death penalty in Nebraska and is engaged in similar efforts in fourteen states, most recently Ohio. *Right Here, Right Now*, while addressing none of the policy arguments that color the current debate—exonerations, serious mental illness, race disparities, costs—attacks the very premise of the penalty: that certain persons are disposable, that they have no humanity the law is obligated to respect. In the last decade, state supreme courts in Connecticut, Washington, and Delaware have invalidated the death penalty as violative of state constitutional protections. In deepest red Kansas, the state supreme court has invited briefing on the question of whether protection of "life and liberty" under Section 1 of the state constitution renders the death penalty unconstitutional. The stories shared in *Right Here, Right Now* poignantly illustrate the myriad ways that society failed to protect and nurture the life and liberty interests of the "hidden voices" while they were children, vulnerable and impressionable—innocents in the fullest sense of the word. The same or similar stories, easily available from the condemned on Kansas's death row, when considered alongside the caprice with which these hidden voices have been selected for extermination, make plain that the court should find the penalty unconstitutional under Kansas law.

American exceptionalism has been under attack for a decade, and the Trump administration, instead of resisting that trend, seemed committed to ceding global leadership to China, Russia, or Europe. Retention of the death penalty separates America from all of Europe and much of Western civilization. In Africa, where American influence on matters political, economic, and cultural still remains strong, countries closely watch American developments in civil and human rights. Last summer I served on the faculty of the Makwanyane Institute, in Cape Town, South Africa, convening sixteen fellows from seven sub-Saharan African countries for advanced training on death penalty litigation and advocacy. The fellows, very appreciative of the efforts of the American faculty, uniformly advised that the most significant help

Americans can provide to opponents of the death penalty on the continent is to abolish the death penalty in the United States. We are getting closer (there were twenty-two executions in 2019, continuing the drop to record-breaking low levels over the past five years), but in the meantime, governments continue to kill their most impaired, vulnerable, and marginalized prisoners. Even as I prepared this foreword, I received two heartbreaking email messages from fellows. One announced, "Six men have been executed this morning in Somaliland. The first executions since 2016." The second, from a Nigerian fellow, reported, "My client has been convicted of murder charge. He's been sentenced to death by hanging. A sad day for me." People of goodwill the world over should be saddened by this news.

Interestingly, the nations represented at the Makwanyane Institute look at the death penalty through an entirely different cultural lens from that which condemned the hidden voices amplified in *Right Here, Right Now*. Without the history of chattel slavery, the Civil War, Reconstruction, and Jim Crow, the death penalty on the continent runs counter to cultural norms native to Africans. Absent is the level of dehumanizing of the prisoner that is a signature of the American prison. African courts and justice institutions are significantly underfunded and generally have shallow footings in procedural and substantive due process. That said, African justice systems, and their laws and practices, are not so entwined in an ideology as pervasive and as toxic as the white supremacy narrative that underlies the American death penalty. The Makwanyane Institute takes its name from the landmark 1995 decision of the Constitutional Court of South Africa that invalidated the death penalty under the interim constitution. If and when the United States joins the enlightened position of South Africa, Europe, and most democracies, abolition in Africa will surely follow in short order.

I reflect over the stories in *Right Here, Right Now* and see two clear calls to action. First, to see and hear the voices of these long-hidden souls, recognize their humanity, and link arms with those individuals and organizations working to abolish the death penalty, the most inhumane of social policies. The question posed at the end of "You Can Be Anything" (chapter 24) is heartbreaking to the core. Yes, a searing *what if?* The second rallying cry I hear bursting forth from this compilation is more proactive: The impaired and broken prisoners, young and old alike, were once vulnerable, needy, worthy of protection. We failed them. Will we fail the children who today find no safe places in their homes, their overcrowded and under-resourced schools; who are living with food and housing insecurity, with parents unable to afford adequate health care? These challenges face us, right here, right now. Will we rise to meet them?

Acknowledgments

To the more than one hundred story sharers, artists, and visionaries who helped develop the Hidden Voices project Serving Life: ReVisioning Justice and who continue to expand its reach today, I extend my profound gratitude and admiration. To the many universities, civic organizations, conferences, galleries, and faith communities that hosted readings of these monologues, installed the exhibits, took up collections, or provided meals and transportation for families, thank you for bringing forward these stories. Thanks also to all the individuals, organizations, and foundations who continue to fund Serving Life as it evolves, including A Blade of Grass; the Fund for Southern Communities; Humanities for the Public Good, UNC–Chapel Hill; the MAP Fund; the North Carolina Arts Council; the Paul Green Foundation; and the Triangle Community Foundation. The work could not exist without your kind support.

In particular, I want to thank those who offered artistic support and visionary direction at crucial moments in the project development: Peter Kuhns, Kathryn Hunter-Williams, Jennifer Thompson, Nancy Demorest, William Paul Thomas, Carlyn Wright-Eakes, Rachel Campbell, Frank Baumgartner, Douglas Campbell, Jon Powell, Vivienne Benesch and PlayMakers Repertory Company, Marc Callahan, Dana Reason, Madeleine Lambert, Richard Lonon, Ann Joyner, Allan Parnell, Michael Betts, Sita Lozoff, Catherine Dumas, Jenny Warburg, Graig Meyer, Jonathan and

Leah Wilson-Hartgrove, Cooper and Noah Harris, Allison Layague, the Center for Death Penalty Litigation, and the North Carolina Coalition for Alternatives to the Death Penalty.

I am indebted to Jayne Ifekwunigwe and stellar editor Gisela Fosado, who imagined this book after hearing a reading at Duke University's Rubenstein Arts Center. Your insights and perspective have been invaluable; all writers should be so fortunate.

Most of all, to Cerron, Chanton, Darrell, Doug, George, Gotti, H.L., Henry, Jas, Jason, Kenneth, KenTay, Leroy, Little Bison, Lump, Lyle, Mr. Blue, Paul, Rico, Rodney, Rome Alone, Stephen, Will, William, and the others: I never cease to be moved by your kind and generous sharing. Heart to heart is the only way to thrive.

To all the family members who so willingly shared their time and stories: your welcoming spirits have been a true blessing.

Finally, to every single person who helped create Serving Life in all its varied forms: your vast compassion, breathtaking talents, and tireless dedication will surely bring the dawn.

Introduction

To the reader, from a man living on death row:

FACT: *Tough guys (like I'm supposed to be) are soft guys too, tenderhearted and caring. We love animals and children very much and cry sometimes when we see images of their suffering. I am not ashamed to say that I like to read* Mother Earth News *magazine. I especially like the last page of the publication, called "Earth Words." This page shows beautiful pictures of natural landscapes accompanied by a poem or some words of wisdom.*

One issue shows a hippopotamus with a portion of its head, eyes, and snout above the water in the Linyanti River at sunset. The accompanying poem is one of Maya Angelou's; it reads: "No sun outlasts its sunset, but will rise again and bring the dawn."

I'm praying that you bring the dawn, God willing.

What does it mean for each of us to bring the dawn? When I was a kid, we would sometimes go camping all alone. Just before sunset, we'd head off with nothing but a tent, sleeping bags, and ourselves. We'd tell ghost stories, stay up late, and if we got hungry, it was easy enough to hunt up something to eat. Easy because we were "camping" in our backyard.

Just before dawn, when the night was its darkest and chilliest, we'd generally abandon the tent for our own warm beds.

Many of those who live on death row didn't have backyards as children, and if they did, those backyards certainly weren't places to safely sleep.

1

And as for hunting up groceries, good luck with that. Too often, there simply weren't any. Even when there was food, it was often kept padlocked in a cabinet or refrigerator, since food was limited and the hunger of growing boys was not. Instead of pretending to camp out, one man recalled how he and his brother pretended to be locked up. Pretended to be incarcerated.

I think about my own children, how they built tepees and forts and treehouses. How they never once played "prison." How they didn't even know what prison was.

In 2013, Hidden Voices was invited by a psychologist, the programs director at a prison, to develop a project for a group of residents living on death row. At that time, the death penalty was lawful in thirty-five states, down one from the previous year after Connecticut abolished its death sentence. More than three thousand people were incarcerated on America's Death Row. And that number didn't even count America's Junior Death Row: the children we sentenced to life without parole, meaning the children we sentenced to grow up and die in prison.

At Hidden Voices, we describe ourselves as "a radically inclusive, participatory, and co-creative collective committed to creating just, compassionate, and sustainable relationships." Building these relationships is the only way to create the just and compassionate world we all wish to inhabit. So I suggested that instead of developing a project *for* the men, we follow our usual process and develop a project *with* the men. At Hidden Voices, our core values are simple: *All lives have meaning. All stories matter*. The programs director agreed. We were in. But little did we imagine what we were in *for*.

When we walked into that first meeting in 2013, we brought nothing but paper, pencils, and our Hidden Voices process. At the close of our second meeting, we left with a list of intended outcomes, a rich visioning of what we might create to achieve those outcomes, and a list of whom to invite to our table: both to speak and to listen.

By unanimous agreement, the most critical intention read like this: "We intend for our stories to break the stereotype of who lives on death row. We want the public to know we are not monsters." And so we set forth with a destination clearly in mind but absolutely no idea how the journey would unfold.

During the following years, we collaborated with those original men, and then others around the country, to create Serving Life: ReVisioning

Justice. The project evolved to include a wealth of material: collections of stories, interviews, performances on death row, cycles of monologues, public readings, two interactive exhibits, and the play *Count: Stories from America's Death Row*. We worked hands-on with groups of men and one-on-one, laughed and wept together on phone calls, exchanged letters, spoke with family members, and invited others living on death row around the country to share their most intimate stories, words, and prayers. The stories in this collection are drawn from those interactions.

The men who played "prison," and who now live there, generally preferred to share stories of the "good times," in no small part because those stories stood in relief against the background chaos: the time they went to an amusement park; the time they got a pair of brand-new shoes; the time they went fishing at the creek and Grandma slipped and lost her wig in the water. Heck, who doesn't enjoy a good laugh? But we also invited them to share the other stories, the ones that required more effort. Those stories—of meals that consisted solely of ketchup crackers, of a parent waking the children in the middle of the night and forcing them to choose which one would receive that night's beating, of learning to tie their shoes and smoke weed at the same age—those were shared more slowly and at greater cost. Often they were introduced with the halting words, "I've never told anyone this before."

More than once, the speaker wept.

In those moments, the other guys sat quietly. Patiently. There was no attempt to console, no attempt to stem the rising waters, no patting someone's back. This was prison, after all. The men offered something far more powerful and healing: the profound respect of allowing another person the space to feel what they were feeling, without any need to have that other person stop feeling so that the rest of us might feel *better*. In that windowless place, there was so much unspoken, of tenderness and grief. Of shared, unshed tears for the children they once were, for the men they had become.

One prisoner commented that he never realized the traumatic things that happened in his life were tragic until he became an adult. "It was just stuff that happened, understand?"

Well, sure. Who notices the water in which we swim, the air we breathe? We don't question the beliefs that drive us, because we don't recognize them as beliefs. We just see them as "what is." You can't question what you don't see. As children, those men were just trying to keep their heads above water.

No other society has imprisoned as many of its own as we do here in the United States. What we hide in the dark obscurity of prisons and jails are real people, shredded by mental illness, violence, abuse, and poverty. As one young man told me, "Poverty and prison go together like Kool-Aid and sugar. Without sugar, you got no Kool-Aid. Without poverty, you got no prison."

Scholars from around the world have referred to our current state of incarceration as "American apartheid." In her February 6, 2009, Children's Defense Fund Child Watch column, Marian Wright Edelman writes, "Incarceration is becoming the new American apartheid and poor children of color are the fodder. . . . Child poverty and neglect, racial disparities in systems that serve children, and the pipeline to prison are not acts of God. They are America's immoral political and economic choices that can and must be changed."

Perhaps we would benefit from our own Truth and Reconciliation process. Who need to tell the truth? Who need to listen? Surely we all do. We need to tell the truth about who it is we incarcerate. We need to tell the truth about why we think it's OK. Too often, what we accept as truth is simply some form of *It must be because it is*. Stay within that circular world, and those statements hold up. You can't see the river till you climb onto the banks. But clamber up, and suddenly the river is defined. It stands out against a larger landscape of possibility.

After a public reading of these monologues, an audience member said, "I always assumed those men must belong on death row because that's where they were." Simple, isn't it? We can't see what we don't know. The muddy waters of those other lived realities are opaque to us.

In one of our prison sessions, a resident stated bluntly that childhood was overrated; he didn't remember "anything positive under all that dirt." Another man gently insisted they shouldn't blame childhood circumstances for their choices. As young teens they had chosen to start selling drugs. No one had forced them. But is that true?

The notion of "choice" has such allure. It is seductive to imagine we are in control of our destinies. But when I asked my children how they might have gone about buying and selling drugs in middle school, they just laughed. The best they could come up with was a girl rumored to have smoked a joint.

My children wouldn't have "chosen" to sell drugs because (1) we didn't need the money and (2) they'd have had no idea where or how to begin. At thirteen, my children were surrounded by ice skates, baseball practice, and violins. The young man who made the comment about "choice" was surrounded by guns, drugs, and an immediate need for rent money. Are we seriously trying to convince ourselves that this boy had the same choices as my kids? That we have acted responsibly by sentencing children like him to execution or to life in prison without parole, meaning to grow up and die there?

The men were shocked to hear me say this. But my goodness, just look around. Who benefits from the conjoined notion of choice and personal responsibility? Obviously, it's those with the most benefits. The story we tell ourselves is we are personally responsible, because of the choices we made, for our abundant benefits, and you are personally responsible for your lack of them. This false narrative enables us to wash our hands of *our* responsibility to fix what is clearly broken. It allows us to ignore what and whom we leave in our wake.

At thirteen, I don't think anyone has much free choice. What we have are our given circumstances. In one conversation, the men compared notes as to the first time they saw someone killed. Think back—how old were you when you witnessed your first murder? The youngest was three. These children, now prisoners, were caught in a net that was not of their making.

When I listened to their stories, one thought arose over and over: it's a wonder any survive at all. That some survive with hearts intact is a damn miracle. Many have never, in all their years in prison, had a single rehabilitative or support program. Some were surprised to know there even were such things. Many men have lived twenty-three hours a day in a small, windowless cell, their food trays pushed through a slot in the door, with only one hour spent outside, and that in a cage. Most of the men have not had a contact visit in decades. They have not hugged their mothers in ten, twenty, thirty years. Have not touched their children, their grandchildren. These men reflect to us the communities of absence in which they were reared, which are our very own shadow communities.

Yet somehow their hearts have expanded beyond their often violent and despairing upbringings, beyond their current deprivations. They want so much to be of service. One man wrote that "sacrifice is not the ending of life but the devotion to it." These men envision a system where they might serve as coordinators of rehabilitative programs, their focus not on freeing themselves but on freeing younger prisoners' minds through the truth of their own stories. They imagine these younger prisoners returning to their neighborhoods and families with a new restorative vision of justice. As one man wrote, "I pray, I hope to give back a bit of what I have taken from the world."

After listening to a public reading of the men's stories, audiences tend to sit silent, stunned.

"What do you feel?" I often ask.

One woman answered, "I just feel shame. For years, I've driven by the prison near where I work without once thinking about who is inside." She teared up. "It makes me wonder what else I've never thought to think about, who else I've overlooked."

Do the stories in this book humanize the men? Certainly. But my hope is that by reading these stories, we humanize ourselves. We need to trouble the waters of our complacency: a complacency that claims those of us gifted with childhoods free from witnessing murders, from the need to sell drugs for rent, from incarcerated parents, aren't indebted to those who were not so fortunate. We are. And we are called to recirculate our unearned good fortune in the form of tangible, hands-on, loving action.

Just like the woman driving by that prison every day, most of us have washed our hands of these men and their families long ago. Yet as I write this, it is Easter and Passover, the season of new life, new beginnings, the coming of a new day of liberation. I have heard that the true meaning of washing one's hands during the seder is not about pretending to some inner purity, but signifying that we are prepared to participate. Without hesitation, we are ready to do whatever is within our reach.

What is within your reach? *Who* is within your reach? We all know some small action we can take in the name of love and compassion and liberation from our own limiting and hidebound perspectives. One small action practiced over and over can free us all.

I leave you with this final story. One of my friends sent big news: two geese had taken up residence in the rec yard. Of all the possible places in the world, this pair had determined that the perfect spot to build a nest was inside a prison compound.

Before long, the men realized that the female had laid a clutch of eggs. "She rarely moved," my friend wrote, "except to adjust the nest and hiss at anyone who got too close. Even the male stayed away, seeming content to walk the yard with the rest of us, a quizzical tilt to his head."

Can't you just imagine the gander as one of the guys, pacing the yard and keeping his distance from a short-tempered partner? No wonder. Nesting is no picnic. The eggs must be gently rotated beneath the mother so that the temperature remains constant and the membranes don't stick to the shells. The mother leaves only to drink and eat. Some of the men, concerned about the overwhelming heat swamping the area, made a little tub to hold water. They sat it where the mother could crane her head and drink without leaving the nest. Each day, when the men were allowed in the yard for their hour, the first thing they checked was whether the mother needed more water. Some carried out bits of bread for her to eat.

Anticipation grew. And on the day the shells broke open and the baby goslings emerged, men who hadn't been outside in twenty years came to see the fuzzy hatchlings, "watching them stumble and bumble around their new surroundings."

Imagine the fresh-born puffballs blinking in the unfamiliar light, surrounded by men who hadn't been outside in decades doing the exact same thing. Amazement all around.

Eventually Animal Control took the birds away.

It was good they were taken, my friend explained. The environment was not conducive to healthy development. Men had spotted hawks, fox pups, even vultures nearby. Were the babies to fledge in that setting, my friend doubted any would survive. Still, the day Animal Control took the geese, my friend said he went outside "and the yard felt like the empty dirt lot it is. Only more so."

It's a gorgeous human quality, this capacity to love beyond boundaries. Animal, human, incarcerated, free. Who knows how or why this happens? It just does. One moment we're encased in our own thick, protective hides, and the next, a miracle occurs and some raw beauty cracks us open. Life catches us off guard, and the light that shines through is shocking. Pink and raw, we suddenly become less who we think we are and more who we truly are: present, tender, welcoming. It dawns on us that the notion of separation is just that: a notion. A ghost story invented by frightened children some dark night.

In those moments of clear seeing, we find ourselves awash in love, connection, community. Our vision of wholeness is restored. If justice rolls like a river, it's surely a river of mercy that carries us all to a shared land where we are washed clean of past ghosts and can wake to a fresh, new day. Truth *is* reconciliation.

These stories will surely break your heart, and that is a fine place from which to view much of what we prefer to keep at arm's length. Handle these stories, these lives, with care. Let the words find a nesting place in your heart. And when the stories crack you open, be glad for the light.

About the Stories

The voices and stories in this volume represent a cross section of the United States, from California to Washington, DC, from Maine to Florida. In addition to the men from those states, we corresponded or spoke with men incarcerated on death rows in Alabama, Arkansas, Colorado, Florida, Indiana, Kansas, Maryland, New York, North Carolina, Ohio, Pennsylvania, South Carolina, Texas, Utah, and Virginia.

The events related in these stories took place during the past six decades. All the men were born between approximately 1960 and 1990. When we began the project, all had been living on death row for more than five years, and some had been incarcerated more than thirty. The youngest participant was in his twenties and the oldest close to sixty.

For reasons of privacy, protection, and security, personal and place names have been removed from the material. This is standard practice for every Hidden Voices project, whether that project focuses on sexual assault, immigration, military experiences, family violence, or any other pressing social issue. There can be very real repercussions for those who speak out, and we assure each participant that we will do our utmost to maintain their anonymity. In the context of this book, the incarcerated men whose voices reach beyond prison walls may experience tangible pushback. We have seen prison programs canceled, phone and recreation privileges suspended, and prisoners moved into solitary confinement after speaking to reporters, posting on a blog, or accessing other means of public communication. For families, too, the stigma associated with death row is very real; we have known families forced to relocate once a loved one was convicted.

There is another reason to omit such identifiers. Specifics such as age, race, and geographic location can allow us as readers to more easily distance ourselves from these experiences. Absent a specific image of the speaker, we more easily and viscerally allow the deeper truth of the story to penetrate.

As mentioned in the introduction, the raw material for these stories came via several avenues. Sometimes the stories were embedded or referenced in longer written pieces. Other times the stories formed the basis for remembrances, poems, letters, essays, or interviews. Sometimes the stories were shared orally, in response to another man's written or spoken reflection. When we met in person with our collaborators, we took copious notes and later asked for clarifications and additional details by mail or during a subsequent workshop. Some men were marvelous writers; others saw themselves more as visual artists; still others cared nothing for writing but did care deeply about the project goals and were gifted storytellers. For some time, we also ran a story slam inside prison, and about forty men participated in those offerings. We recorded and transcribed telephone conversations with the men and their families, and from those conversations, we excerpted comments, details, and dialogue that illuminated important themes. Through the generosity of a well-respected prison magazine, we were able to send a broad national request for any stories, poems, and prayers that death row residents wished to share with a public audience. We received almost a hundred responses. This abundance of material allowed us to create the varied components of Serving Life: ReVisioning Justice.

There was great commonality in many of the men's experiences, and a few times, the stories were so similar that it was hard to distinguish one from the other. While we couldn't include but one such story in the collection, we also didn't want to exclude critical details essential to a reader's understanding, so in a few instances, we created a single composite story made richer by those inclusions.

Certainly, the most important thing to remember is simply that all the experiences and incidents shared in the collection are true and happened to real men living on America's Death Row. We are deeply grateful for the vulnerability and generosity these men evinced in sharing some very difficult experiences. It was not easy. It came at a cost. Most everyone on death row suffers from post-traumatic stress. At times, the price for sharing these memories was tangible: nightmares, depression, stress, withdrawal. The men persevered. They did so because they believed the benefit might outweigh the cost. They trusted us when we said there would be an audience who cared—about them, their lives, their families. Most crucially, they trusted that facing their own painful memories might prevent someone else ending up in their situation.

Finally, it is common for people to ask, "Why death row?"

On one level, the answer is simple: that's where we were invited. But there exists a more essential reason: death row is a microcosm of the prison population in our over-incarcerated nation. Almost all residents are low wealth. They are disproportionately racial and ethnic minorities. Mental illness is rampant. Hundreds who were innocent have been convicted, yet even if these men are not "guilty," they're easily perceived as "not innocent enough."

As Bryan Stevenson reminds us in *Just Mercy: A Story of Justice and Redemption*, "Proximity has taught me some basic and humbling truths, including this vital lesson: Each of us is more than the worst thing we've ever done."

Clearly, proximity is key. Proximity to our own failings, to our own innocences and guilts. But what does proximity even mean when we speak of these others, of men who have lived in solitary confinement for years, sometimes decades; men for whom visitors are a rarity and phone calls simply a memory? How do we find proximity to them?

As we collaborated with men living on death row or sentenced as children to die in prison, we conceived the notion of a community call and response between the public and these most hidden members of our society. This collection of stories is one piece of that call. The response, of course, is up to you. We welcome your own stories and correspondence and will share those with the men and their families.

Finally, this collection does not intend to offer a comprehensive overview or critique of our current system of incarceration. Our intent is more limited and personal. Over the past two decades, many excellent books have been written that address the historical roots and policies that have led to our current criminal justice system and our present state of mass incarceration. Consider some of these excellent and compelling resources:

Are Prisons Obsolete? by Angela Y. Davis

Charged: The New Movement to Transform American Prosecution and End Mass Incarceration, by Emily Bazelon

Deadly Justice: A Statistical Portrait of the Death Penalty, by Frank R. Baumgartner, Marty Davidson, Kaneesha R. Johnson, Arvind Krishnamurthy, and Colin P. Wilson

End of Its Rope: How Killing the Death Penalty Can Revive Criminal Justice, by Brandon L. Garrett

Locked In: The True Causes of Mass Incarceration—and How to Achieve Real Reform, by John F. Pfaff

Locking Up Our Own: Crime and Punishment in Black America, by James Forman Jr.

"The New Asylums" (PBS *Frontline* episode), by Miri Navasky and Karen O'Connor

The New Jim Crow: Mass Incarceration in the Age of Colorblindness, by Michelle Alexander

What this book does offer are first-person stories from those most impacted by this system. As you read, you will notice some unmistakable themes: racism, segregation, housing insecurity, underfunded and inadequate educational opportunities, a lack of mental health support, substance abuse, violence, post-traumatic stress syndrome. If you pay attention, you will see these themes reappearing throughout the stories, as the young children grow into young men maturing inside our jails and prisons. This pattern, in which these adverse childhood factors lead to incarceration, has been called the "poverty-to-prison pipeline," the "cradle-to-prison pipeline," and the "school-to-prison pipeline." Whatever label we choose, our work must be to disrupt the pattern and heal the underlying causes.

We decided at the inception of this collection not to include scholarly reflections or commentary on the stories shared. We wanted to offer these voices the space and the respect they deserve; we wanted to offer readers the same. Each reader will find their own pathway into perspective, understanding, and connection. And for those readers eager to engage in healing the harm caused on all sides by our criminal justice system and to restore kindness, compassion, and wholeness across our communities, we have ended the book with a list of solutions-oriented resources, from restorative practices to global alternatives to our current carceral settings.

The Part That Was Innocent

(EARLY CHILDHOOD, BIRTH TO FIVE YEARS OLD)

Playing Solitary

Here's the first game I remember playing. We lived in a one-bedroom apartment. If my baby brother and I woke up and Mom wasn't home from the club, I'd pour us both some Frosted Flakes. Then we'd empty our tiny closet, set the TV in the doorway, climb inside, and hunch over our cereal, watching cartoons. Know what we called the game?

Playing "Solitary."

Man, the first time I went to prison I was only three months old. My mom took me to visit my father. Shoot, not just my father, everybody—grandmas, aunts, uncles, even my mom finally—they all did time. Prison was a family reunion.

As a little kid, I knew the saying "snitches get stitches." I knew the weak get robbed for their property. I remember waking up after a city-wide blackout to find our apartment full of looted merchandise, courtesy of the "five-finger discount." By the time I was six, I was stealing plums from the produce market. What a treat for a kid whose family couldn't afford luxuries like fresh fruit!

First time my mom came to visit *me* in prison, she just stood, looking around, like, "ain't nothing change." It was the same prison where she'd brought me to visit my father.

Yeah. "Ain't nothing change." Trust me, I was a convict long before I ever did time.

Grandma Shot Bob

My very first memory ever is a gun. I was two years old and playing with my Starship *Enterprise* in my grandmother's kitchen. She and her boyfriend Bob were arguing. When I looked up to see what the commotion was about, he slapped her.

Grandma reached into her bathrobe pocket, but he grabbed her arm and they tussled. Suddenly there was a loud pop.

Bob howled, grabbed his foot, and starting cursing. "Gotdammit, Rose, you fuckin' shot me."

I guess she couldn't get the gun out and just shot straight through the pocket.

My nine-year-old cousin came rushing in. Grandma gave her the nickel-plated .38 and told her to hide it in the basement of the building.

"And take the baby with you. Stay there till I come get you."

Talk about excited; not only had Grandma just shot Bob, we were going somewhere new: the basement!

I had no idea what was going on. Except Grandma was trying to not get in trouble. It was a lesson I never forgot: "Don't get caught!"

Ajar

The day I learned about love, the sun was shining and everybody at our whole trailer park was outside. My mom was already over at my auntie's. They sold liquor on the side to help make ends meet. I knew my auntie's friend Charles would be there, too. I liked Charles. He'd lift me over his head and spin me around, saying, "Little man be flyin'!"

But first things first. I was stopping by Ms. Rosie's trailer for my sugar fix. Ms. Rosie was about a hundred and forty years old and wore a Shirley Temple wig that was always just a little crooked.

All of a sudden, this loud *POP* ricocheted across the trailer park.

"It's a backfire," Ms. Rosie explained. "Cars do it."

Then four more blasts. *Pop, pop, pop, pop!*

I took off running. All I could think about was my mother.

We were almost to my aunt's trailer when my uncle's blue Chevy flew by, kicking up gravel and nearly smashing a parked car. Our eyes met. I raised my hand to wave, but he didn't even slow down.

Confused, I tore around the corner. The trailer door was ajar. I climbed the first step and heard the faint music inside. On the second step my tiny hand pushed the bottom of the door, opening it wider. I never made it inside.

Charles was lying on the floor, his shades twisted above his head, a pool of liquid gathering beneath him. My auntie was sprawled across

Charles like a blanket. In the center of her forehead, a round mark was oozing red. Inside the trailer, my mom started to scream and scream.

I just stood there in a stupor, saying over and over, "Get up, Auntie, please get up!"

I think a part of me is standing there still, on that step. The part that was innocent and hadn't yet learned that love kills.

No Questions Asked

It was the most exciting night of my three-year-old life. Two teenage girls were fighting, and a crowd had gathered to watch. One of the girls was my mother.

My baby brother had just been born, and his father and my moms had been arguing. He didn't want her to take the baby home with us. Somehow his sister got involved. That's who my moms was fighting.

Suddenly, a white Lincoln Continental screeched to the curb. It belonged to my grandmoms's boyfriend. The doors popped open, and out they jumped like Bonnie and Clyde.

Now, my grandmoms is a little woman—four feet, eleven inches—but she seemed like a giant with that pearl-handled Saturday night special. Her boyfriend had a big Afro and a long switchblade just like Daddy Cool. I was in awe.

The crowd backed away, then dispersed. The girls stopped fighting.

My grandmoms was in a seething rage. "You better go get my grandson *right* now," she told the father. Then she turned to my moms. "And you better beat that bitch ass."

Grandmoms scooped me up and put me in the car. Looking out the window, I watched while my moms did exactly that.

No one explained, but I understood. You back up family without question and by any means necessary. My grandmoms was ready to kill someone if she had to. No questions asked.

Downpour

Growing up in my house was a fucking horrific, crazy, sad experience. I remember this one cinder-block house we lived in. Man, the windows busted out and covered with plastic. If we wanted warm water, we had to heat it on the stove.

And my dad, he beat my mom all the time. Then they'd make up. I hated that shit.

Now, this is very personal. We were living in that cinder-block shack, and this one night when my baby brother was about a month old, Dad beat my mom up. Then he told Mom to get the hell out of the house and take us kids with her. Thing is, it was one in the morning and we didn't have anywhere else to go. Plus, it was raining, not a hard downpour, but a steady drizzle. So we huddled up under this huge oak tree. Mom held the baby and I clung to her side while she covered us with her jacket the best she could. We stayed under that tree till dawn.

When it was light, Mom gave me the baby to hold while she went to check if Dad had passed out from being drunk so we could go back inside. I tried to keep the baby warm, but by nighttime he was sick. He caught pneumonia and died in his crib one night not even a week later.

Thing is, nobody, to this very day, has ever mentioned anything about what happened. But I didn't forget. I used to go to his grave site and put flowers by the little headstone. Soon as I was old enough, I got his initials tattooed on my left arm. So I always carry him with me in memory.

I wonder sometimes what our lives would have been like if he had lived. Whether my other brother and me would have lived different lives than becoming addicts.

I don't know. When you're a kid, you don't got perspective. You just got bruises.

Nigger Lover

First time I ever saw a gun, my grandma was holding it. I heard a ruckus in the hallway and peeked out my door. Grandma was holding a tiny pistol, so small it was almost hidden in her hand. I was too little to understand she'd been drinking. All I knew was Grandma had a gun! The same Grandma who was the sweetest woman in the whole wide world. The same Grandma who, whenever Mama said, "Absolutely not!" always said, "Of course you can, baby."

Grandma was cussing at Mama's bedroom door, saying, "I'm gonna shoot that goddamn nigger." I'd never heard her say such awful words.

Mama opened her door and calmly said, "Give me the gun."

But Grandma kept waving the gun and cussing. So Mama said, "If you're gonna shoot anybody in this house, you're gonna have to shoot me first."

I was so terrified Grandma was gonna shoot Mama I didn't know what to do.

Finally, Grandma lowered the pistol, muttering, "Nigger lover."

I sat on my bed, tears spilling down my cheeks. I was part black. I didn't understand that Grandma was drunk and talking about my white mother and another man. I thought she was saying my mother was wrong for loving *me*.

I sat there for a long time, wondering why black people were called niggers and how come we weren't supposed to be loved.

Shelf Life

I was four when my father started trying to kill me. We never knew when it was going to happen. My mother would be working a night shift at the hospital, and my father might come home in that crazy mode. My brothers and sisters tried to protect me, telling him I was at my godparent's house. But there wasn't much they could do. He'd search the house until he found where they had hidden me—stashed in a toy box, or tucked between the covers of someone's bedding, or under a pile of clothes on a shelf.

Once my father found me, he would very gently pick me up, hold me close, and carry me to the bathroom, speaking softly of things I never understood. About my mother, I think. How maybe I wasn't his son. All the while the tub would be filling with hot water. Then he'd wrap my face and head in a towel, and in what seems now like an almost ministerial act, he'd dunk my head into the tub.

The attacks got more and more intense. He wouldn't be satisfied until I'd sucked in enough water to piss and soil myself and pass out.

I learned to survive. But what does that even mean? By the time I got to be six, I'd become—hell, I don't know what I'd become.

This is what I do know. I clearly remember it being a Sunday. Close to 5:00 p.m., because my mother was getting ready for a night shift at the hospital. I remember feeling like that night he could drown me for real.

So I set our living room on fire.

I didn't run from the room. It was fully ablaze, but I wasn't scared. In that moment, I was fine with whatever results I got.

We never lived with my father again. But within a year, my mother had made another really bad choice.

I realize now my father wasn't trying to kill me. I was just a little child; if he'd wanted to kill me, he could have. It wasn't attempted murder. It was torture.

8

Not the Worst Fate

My childhood, it started off very violent. I had to fight from a very early age—this is from two or three. One of my earliest memories is going out to play with other children and someone throwing me into one of those big apartment dumpsters. I was maybe two years old. It was hot outside, so it was really hot in the dumpster. And I remember crying and screaming, but no one came. I don't know how long I was in there before someone found me.

We would have to pretty much fight every day to go to school on the bus and then fight to walk home from the bus stop. In the neighborhood we lived in, this became a routine. You'd have to fight your way into the neighborhood. If you wanted to be accepted, you'd have to fight your way to that acceptance. If you weren't accepted, you'd have to fight because of that. We basically lived in a children's open war zone, which could be very, very cruel.

My mother and father also fought a lot. They'd sit up arguing all night, until they'd get to the point where they couldn't talk, and they'd just start fighting physically. And my father, he'd beat my mother. It was like this for the whole time they were together. So my childhood was chaos, chaos with no breaks.

I was scared, afraid of the dark like any typical kid. Afraid of monsters in my closet. But the fears, they resonated with where I was from. Because the fear where I was from is real. We heard gunshots, saw dead bodies of people laying on the ground, shot. You figured you could get cut anytime, so the fear was real for me.

Those were the first things that sort of formed my mind. Violence wasn't anything that I looked for or that I initiated; we were just forced into it. Violence was just a response to the environment in order to survive, just adapting to these extreme behaviors. We had to deal with a lot of things that my parents didn't help me cope with in any way. They never taught me certain things that they should have. They just did their best with what they had, to keep me alive, basically. But it wasn't well enough to protect me or show me how to deal with the real world. Because my world was small. It was just my neighborhood. That's the only world I ever saw, and it was vicious.

My father, he would also beat me and my brother a lot. To try and discipline us. I guess that was his way of raising children. A lot of physical abuse. A lot of verbal abuse. The verbal abuse and the physical abuse, it got to some of our teachers. I had a few teachers who tried to intervene. Because they saw I didn't have but two shirts, only had flip-flops for shoes, that sort of thing. One teacher realized I was behind not because I couldn't learn, but because I'd never had the opportunity *to* learn. She really went the extra mile. But she just didn't have the option of giving me more options. I lived where I lived, and I belonged to my mother. When she took me home with her, she still had to take me back. She'd say, "I don't have any choice but to do what your mother says to do, and you have to go home." There were people who would say, "I love you and you should be safe," but they couldn't actually *do* anything.

A few times, authorities were contacted and would come in and take pictures. I guess somebody somewhere was deciding whether we were safe or not. But nothing ever changed. I remember wondering, *Why is this happening?* Nobody being concerned, nobody helping me. Being mad that these things would happen to me. I grew up never feeling safe and never having help. Nobody could save me. I was just on my own.

I think if someone had intervened and taken us out of that situation, my life would be very different today. I think that if I ever had a place that I was safe, a place where I could go and develop as a child, maybe, *maybe* I wouldn't be here. But that never happened. Nobody ever intervened and made the decision to stop this stuff.

I hate to say it, but I think the way that I was raised, the way that I was born, the community that I was born into, I think that those things sort

Not the Worst Fate

of *destined* me to go to prison. Some people ask, "Why doesn't everybody that comes from there go to prison?" Well, many, maybe most, do. But that's not the only fate that you can suffer from those circumstances. And it's not even actually the worst fate you can suffer. My brother deals with a lot of mental health issues because we were raised in the same household. A lot of issues that he still deals with to this day. In some ways, his mental health issues are maybe worse than the fate that I've suffered over my twenty years in prison.

9

Car Ride

I was almost five years old and it was a hot summer afternoon. I was playing barefoot on the banks of a ditch and was covered from head to toe in red dirt and dust.

Momma yelled, "Put them dawgs in the car. We takin' 'em for a ride!"

I was excited! I loved our dogs, and we'd never taken them for a ride before. But I was also on alert. Momma had told me plenty of times to stop playing around that ditch, so this might be a trap.

One of our dogs, Ernestine, was a German shepherd and collie mix, black, tan, and white, big and beautiful! Our other dog, Brownie, was smaller, a terrier. He'd been run over by a car and had only one good hind leg.

I called for them while I kept an eye out for Momma. When they came, I ushered the dogs into the back seat of Momma's four-door Ford.

"Come on, y'all, git in!"

For two dogs that had never been in Momma's car before, they seemed to understand exactly what to do. Tails wagging, they jumped in, and I jumped in behind them.

So, off we went on this ride: me, Momma, my sister, and our two dogs. Me and the dogs were in the back seat having a ball! They were jumping all over me, licking me in my face. Momma would usually say, "Stop lettin' them damn dawgs lick you in the face, fool!" But not today.

After riding for a while, we were deep out in the wood, just red oak and pine trees and long country roads. Suddenly, Momma stopped the car in the middle of the road, and I thought, "Uh-oh!" I wasn't sure if she'd had enough of me and the dogs having fun in the back seat or if this was about me playing around that ditch. Either way, I figured I was about to get a beating.

Instead, Momma said, "Open the door and let them dawgs out."

I did as I was told. I hopped out and called for the dogs, "Come on, y'all, git out!"

But they didn't move. They looked at me as if to say, "Boy, you must be crazy! We ain't gittin' outta this car!"

But then they jumped out, tails wagging. Momma got out, too, and told me to get back in. She closed my door. And sped off.

Looking out the back window, I could see Ernestine and Brownie desperately trying to catch us. But with only three legs, Brownie couldn't run fast. And Ernestine, maternal protector that she was, wouldn't leave him behind.

"Momma, please stop!" I cried over and over again, but she wouldn't. And just like that, our dogs were gone, faded over a hill in the distance.

I can't recall ever crying and screaming like that again in my life. Tears, snot, slobber, and sweat covered both me and the back seat. The red dust made my tears and sweat look like blood. I was crying so hard that I could barely breathe. Eventually, I cried myself to sleep.

I never knew why Momma did that. What did the dogs do wrong? All I knew was Momma left our dogs way out there in the middle of the woods with nothing to eat or drink. And she did it with absolutely no regrets. I couldn't help but wonder, if I were really bad, would she do me the same way?

10

Momma's Boy

I wanted them dead.

Both of 'em.

My mother was a high school dropout, but between welfare checks and the occasional menial job, she kept a roof over our heads and food on the table. Most of the time.

I remember, when I was four, an older cousin trying to teach me how to tie my shoes. It was hard 'cause we'd been playing cards and smoking weed.

My mom enjoyed the fast life. I can't count how many times we were left alone while she went out to a club. She'd put us to bed and tell us not to answer the door or telephone. Even at that young age, I knew the horrible things that could happen if we did.

Sometimes she didn't come home. No problem. I grew up fast, learning how to do for me and my brother. At five, I knew how to boil eggs, mix them with mayo, and make egg salad. I could fry eggs and bacon to near perfection.

OK, maybe not perfection, but we never died, right?

Occasionally we watched TV with my mother, but that was about it for closeness. We didn't even eat dinner with her. Ever. We got a hug on our birthday or some other special occasion, but most of my physical contact with her came when she was whipping me. I got more whippings than I can count. Many because of my brother. He was a crybaby, a tattle-tale, and clearly my mother's favorite.

I didn't like being beat. It made me cry, and crying was for "momma's boys," the ones who grew up to be "homos." My mother's boyfriend also beat me. I don't know how that shit started, but I hated it. He had no right to put his hands on me. But my mother allowed it.

By the time I was five, I hated both my mother and my brother. I don't remember the date or even the time of year; I just remember waking up in the middle of the night wanting them dead. I had suffered enough. With them gone, I could get a *new* family. The kind you saw on TV, the kind who loved each other. The kind who protected each other.

All I needed was a knife.

The bathroom light was on because my brother was afraid of the dark. Truth be told, I was still afraid of the dark, too, but I would never have admitted it. I was a boy. A bad boy.

I climbed out of bed and tiptoed to the kitchen for the butcher knife. I knew what to do—I had seen it all on television. Of course, I was scared. I was too young for prison, but there were other places I could be sent, and I didn't want that to happen. That would ruin my plan to get a new family.

I stood there, waiting, for the longest time. Finally, I returned the knife to the dish rack and went back to bed.

11

Good Habits

I grew up very, very poor. Roaches and rats, spiders, and any insect that could wander into the apartment was probably there. When I walked out of our apartment, everybody would be standing around doing drugs. And there was all this trash—the ground would be littered with alcohol bottles. Broken glass and needles everywhere. And I would be barefoot, walking outside, wanting to play.

I didn't know any other way to live. I saw families and other children on TV, and they have a father and they have a mother, they're eating dinner, they're out having fun. I just knew *that's not us*. That's not our family. I knew this at a very young age. I knew we were poor. Because even to the poor people, which was everyone in our neighborhood, we were poor.

I think the fact that both my mother and my father struggled with drugs, it contributed greatly to our finances. We had a lot of needs that could have been met had we had the money. But we never did.

My mother, when I was born, she had a drinking problem. And throughout my childhood, she was always smoking weed and doing cocaine. My mother had mental health issues that being a child you can't recognize, you don't know. So she was very erratic in her behavior. She dealt with a lot of depression, a lot of anxiety. I don't think my mother wanted to have kids, to not be able to live life, to go out and do things.

My parents basically worked at whatever jobs they were able to scrape together. And that wound up with us just having a lot of needs. We received the bare minimum of things. I don't know that it was their fault—I think they did the best they could. But we would have to eat breakfast and lunch at school, and at certain times, we'd have to skip meals because we didn't have any food.

My mom, she would make up different ways that we could eat. She would work at a fast food restaurant so she could bring home food. We would go over to people's houses and eat there, or visit family members at meal times so we could have lunch or dinner with them.

I don't remember being hungry exactly, but I do remember that when we ate, it was important to eat it all, because we didn't know when we would eat next. We didn't know when we would have food. Food wasn't something that we had regularly and could depend on. We couldn't just go in the refrigerator and get whatever we wanted. Sometimes, there was only a box of baking soda, an onion, and maybe some water in there.

So I grew up very hungry without even realizing it. Which meant I had very, very little in the way of good eating habits. Or any good habits at all.

Boot Camp

(ELEMENTARY SCHOOL,
SIX TO TEN YEARS OLD)

12

It Was Reefer

Drugs and alcohol were the house music of our lives. Before I was born, my father was sent to prison for trafficking heroin. When I was five, I watched my stepdad die from alcohol convulsions. I remember my aunt clinching a belt between her teeth, trying desperately to find a vein for her heroin. But reefer, that was my mother's trade. She'd stuff little brown envelopes with enough reefer to roll three nice-sized joints, which she called nickel bags. Soon she graduated to dime bags and twenty-cent pieces. I knew them all as I watched her weigh and measure the reefer into sandwich bags.

She kept the ready-to-sell merchandise in the kitchen cabinet right behind the coffee. Sometimes when a customer came to the house, she'd send me to get the merchandise so the customer wasn't left unattended. I liked going to get those bags. It made me feel important. It made me feel proud. Even though I was only six, I was responsible! My mother trusted me.

I knew selling reefer was illegal because my mother stressed how important it was not to tell anyone or we'd get in trouble. But I knew my mother wasn't a bad person, so I couldn't see what was bad about it. I loved reefer. I loved the way it smelled and the effect it had on my mother! It was reefer that bought us video games. Reefer that put carpet on the floor. Reefer that kept my mother from being too mad when I got into trouble.

And best of all, it was reefer that was going to get us out of the projects and into a nice house.

One night when we were asleep, someone broke into our apartment and stole all the reefer from the kitchen cabinet. That was the final straw. For the first time, my mother was truly afraid. What if one of her kids had woke up in the middle of the night and walked in on a burglary? Forget nickel and dime bags, Mom started selling half ounces. That's when I learned she was also selling cocaine. My mother was going to get us out of the projects, and she was going to do it fast.

Within a year, she had.

13

Blistered

I know the exact moment I realized my father was off the chain. He and his sister were celebrating a visit from their brother. Seven of us little kids were sprawled in front of my aunt's TV watching a cartoon movie. The place was littered with potato chip bags, wads of napkins, toy cars, red plastic party cups—all of it, including us, layered with hamburger grease, ketchup, and blue icing.

It was a perfect Saturday evening.

My dad was, um, "borrowing" my aunt's bedroom. Even with our cartoon blaring, we could still hear him and some lady friend behind the closed door. Over at the wet bar, my aunt was spilling drinks with her brother and passing their special cigarette back and forth. Her hair was sticky with sweat from the summer heat and Jack Daniels. My uncle had taken off his shirt and tucked it in his back pocket.

Suddenly, the front door opened and in walked my aunt's big, burly husband, Bobby Cain.

Instantly, he zeroed in on the noises coming from his bedroom. He practically tore the door off its hinges as he crashed through. Then he turned and ripped loose our TV and smashed it against my dad's naked, hairy back.

In the time it took my dad to pull on his pants, Cain grabbed a sawed-off shotgun from the hall closet and started walking forward, gun pointed at my dad's belly. It was the first time I ever saw a gun pointed at a human being.

My uncle pulled out a hawkbill knife and warned, "You know if you kill my brother, I'm gonna have to kill you."

Bobby Cain just said, "I got two barrels."

My aunt was sobbing. The seven of us kids were bawling, but my dad just looked at Bobby Cain and said real quiet, "Don't kill me in front of my kids."

Bobby Cain paused a moment, then motioned my dad out the door.

My aunt tried to hold us back, but we scooted past her into the yard. Bobby Cain and my dad stood there staring at each other for what seemed like forever, the sky behind them red and blistered. My uncle crouched between them, knife raised.

Then Bobby Cain pulled the trigger.

Click.

Everyone jumped. He thrust the gun forward as he pulled the trigger again.

Click.

My dad sprang up, latched onto Bobby Cain's throat and crotch, and slammed him onto the ground. Then he straddled the body, pounding left, right, left, right, over and over, smashing him between the eyes with a sound like raw steak slapping concrete.

My uncle tried to stop him. "It's over. It's done. Stop. You're gonna kill him. Your kids are watching!" And finally, "*His* kids are watching."

That did it. You could see the fight drain out of my dad. He turned to us, his shaking fists and heaving chest soaked with Bobby Cain's blood. "Get in the car."

For years after that, I was numb. When my dad beat us, I was petrified and compliant. I had seen what he was capable of. He had nearly killed a grown man with his bare hands. He could sure as heck kill us.

14

Ode to a Pretty Girl

I didn't dare talk to her; I was much too shy for that. Besides, I was eight and Michelle was thirteen. Had I told her I thought she was pretty, she probably would have laughed, or made fun of me. I didn't want to take that chance. I noticed her, though.

She had a brother, maybe a year or two younger. He was one of the tougher boys in the neighborhood. I'd see him for a few months, then hear he was in juvenile detention or reform school for stealing or robbing someone. I couldn't ever remember seeing him smile. I sure didn't want to have to fight him if I somehow offended his sister.

Their mother drank with the guys on the corner. She'd have seizures, and the men would have to hold her down until the paramedics arrived to keep her from hurting herself. I thought she was a nice lady when she wasn't drinking, but she seemed to always be drinking whenever I saw her.

One day, I was sitting on the front porch and saw Michelle, her mother, and her brother arguing. It was a heated exchange, with lots of threatening gestures. Michelle called her mother a bitch. Her brother unleashed two ferocious closed-fist punches to Michelle's face. She collapsed.

I sat there, horrified. He said, "Don't ever call my mother a bitch." Then, to my astonishment, he and their mother just walked off, leaving Michelle there on the ground, hurt and crying.

I wanted to run to her. I wanted to tell her things would be all right. She seemed so alone. But growing up in an ultraviolent environment, I had learned early one of life's most important lessons: "Mind your own business." So I just sat there, saying nothing.

The image of her lying on the ground stayed with me. But there were violent incidents nearly every day. When I went to school, it was with the fear of who I'd have to fight. When we played after school, the drug dealers were always on the corner.

Sometimes there would be gunshots. We learned to not even look, just hit the ground. It didn't matter if there was motor oil, broken glass, or urine where you were standing; at the sound of gunfire, you hit the ground. It was instinct.

Whenever I went to the store, there was always the threat of older boys wanting to rob me. I eventually put the thought of Michelle out of my mind.

A few years later, when I was maybe twelve, I was hanging out with some boys. I knew I had no business being out so late, but I was almost a teenager. One of the boys said, "Hey, look there."

And there was Michelle. She was a working girl. I couldn't believe it. I got butterflies in my stomach, same as when I was a kid, but this time, I was also sad.

She looked nice in her miniskirt and high heels, though a bit awkward. She looked much better in jeans and T-shirts. And she had on makeup, which she didn't need. The guys started making cat calls at her. I think she was embarrassed. We'd all grown up together. She just rolled her eyes. I averted mine.

A few years later, I heard she'd died from a heroin overdose. By then, though, I'd become desensitized to it all. I was convinced that life made no sense, no sense at all.

I know it's naive to wish I'd said something to her. I was just a little ghetto boy. I had nothing to offer. I couldn't have protected her. . . .

But I could have at least told her she was pretty.

But I never said a word.

U-Turn

I was a straight-A student and proud of it! It was pretty much the only thing I had to be proud of. My father was a single parent and schizophrenic. Our home had burned to the ground, destroying everything we weren't wearing. So we'd landed in the projects, where even the playground was littered with crack pipes, broken bottles, and bullet shells. My heart and back were littered, too, from my father's beatings.

Still, my teachers always said if you worked hard, you could be anything. I believed I had a chance to escape the black-hole gravity of poverty. I would stand strong.

Then our fourth-grade class was assigned an essay project. I wrote diligently. The teacher told us to display our work on a trifold board. I told her my family couldn't afford one. My father called her, too. But she said it wouldn't be fair to the other students to make an exception. So she failed me. Which meant I got my first ever C on my report card.

I felt cheated. And hurt. And deeply ashamed. That was the moment I realized hard work didn't matter. Poverty would win out in the end. My dream of being something—somebody—died.

That C was my U-turn.

The Monster

My mom didn't want me to go trick-or-treating. She was worried about my safety in our neighborhood after dark. But after a little pleading and a whole lot of whining, she relented. So my friends and I fanned out into the surrounding neighborhoods, ready for adventure.

I loved my mask. I remember my breath hot against the cheap plastic where my nostrils never matched the holes for your nose. The space for my lips was too small, but I licked the edge and loved the feel of it scrubbing roughly against my tongue. I peered through the eyes of my scary mask with a twinge of excitement pulsing in my chest. I was a monster! With my mask, I was no longer a scared, insecure biracial boy for others to pick on. For one night a year, I would cause others to flee.

As we neared another neighborhood, we could see other trick-or-treaters going door-to-door. My friends approached a group of kids a few years younger than us, snatched their bags of treats, and pushed them down to the dirt.

I heard the younger kids' cries as my friends took off running and laughing. I felt so confused, so angry and hurt. Why were my friends being mean to the other little kids? Why were they stealing when the candy was free?! That made no sense.

It reminds me that once upon a time I was innocent.

I had no idea that in ten short years people would look at my bare face and think, "Monster."

Don't Bring a Gun to a Knife Fight

This was the kind of guy when he comes by everyone holds their head down. In other words, he had a name.

Well, this other dude, who also had a name, took the first guy's bike. The first guy confronted him, saying, "You know my name."

The dude started talking smack, and the first guy said, "You ride on home, and next time you come back, you know my name."

The dude rode on home and got a knife. The first guy went inside and got a gun and sat on his porch, waiting for the dude to show back up. Which he did—the dude pulled right up to the fence and was like, "What's up."

So, the first guy went down there and was running his mouth, and soon as the dude got within striking distance, he cut a hole in the guy. That's why I never believed the "don't take a knife to a gun fight." Because the dude put a nice little hole in the guy.

I remember standing there watching him after he was cut. Even with the streetlights on, I didn't go home. I stood there for so long my mom had to come get me, and she was like, "What are you looking at?"

This lady walked up and said, "He's hurt bad. He probably won't make it."

"What's that towel sticking out of him?" I asked. Every time he breathed you could see this bunched-up towel sticking in and out of him. That's why I was so fascinated.

And she was like, "No, that's his guts."

After that, my mother clawed her way up to a neighborhood where I didn't have to worry all the time. Where if you wanted to see the police, you actually had to call them. I was just starting to relax in life when she fell out of work and we had to move back to the hood.

I was terrified. I told her, "I can't go back. I won't make it." I kept seeing this picture in my head from when I was little, watching this dude take another guy's bike and then cutting his guts out.

They both had a name. And you gotta protect your name 'cause it protects you. But I didn't want a name. I didn't want to have to mess with the likes of them. But in the hood, you got no other choice.

18

Red, Half-White, and Blue

Fear clenched my teeth.
Lips trapped my whimpers when our father beat us.
The lightest sound made jackhammers of his fists,
his leather belt a whip that snapped our pleas to pieces.

My brothers and I winced out of shirts and pants,
comparing backs and hips decorated with blue bruises and red stripes,
testament to our dad's tours of duty,
our dad, who'd been taken captive
by an army of enemy voices in his head.

Even through the rage we could hear the rattling bamboo bars
behind his eyes, raining pain on his half-white children.
Sometimes he'd win his private post-traumatic wrestling match,
break the cage. Then he'd gather us together
in a hug that asked us to understand.
We did: our father was ours
to protect.

So, our pillows swallowed untold secrets,
broken bones were blamed on bikes,
long sleeves and jeans concealed the truth
no matter the season.

It was only when my throat was crushed,
my feet swinging feebly in the air,
that I had sense enough to break
not bones
but this complicated code of silence
and call Child Protective Services.

My father confessed.
The Child Protectors agreed.

I must have deserved it.

The clues were everywhere for anyone
who wished to solve the mystery
of why our family tree was falling in the forest.
But if no one's there to listen:
even the loudest screams fail
to make a sound.

Badge of Honor

It was maybe the first lesson I learned. "Somebody put they hands on you, you hit they ass back. If they bigger than you, get a bottle or stick or somethin'."

My mother's boyfriend was in the navy. One night her voice woke me up. I could tell she was upset. I looked out the trailer window and saw them arguing. He hit her, and they started fighting. Next thing I knew, I was out there in the middle of it, swinging and kicking.

Now, I was only nine and less than half his size, so I know I didn't hurt him. But I must have annoyed him because—*wham!*—he punched me in the face, knocking me to the ground.

My mother screamed, "You hit my son!" and that was the end of the fight, if not the fighting.

But my mom took great pride in telling everyone that her son—a mere kid—was brave enough to fight a grown man.

Later, at ten, I chased my stepfather out of the house with a knife. So I started to get a reputation. And I wore that respect like a badge of honor.

Boot Camp

My dad was a beefy man, built like a human-sized gorilla. My mom was a tiny, delicate-looking woman, which was deceptive. My dad's top four front teeth were false. He'd made the mistake of calling her a bitch during an argument, and her foot instantly shot up to kick that word back down his throat. This was before she left us.

Our dilapidated apartment complex consisted of a hundred units, and my dad was always feuding with some neighbor or another. We kids were my dad's little soldiers, enlisted for his missions. In addition to slicing tires, shattering windows, and setting booby traps on doors using gallon-sized ziplock bags filled with human waste for the parents, I was also sent to fight other kids. We were the only nonblack family in the projects, and my dad wanted our family to give as good as we got.

He made us watch *Full Metal Jacket* so he could point out the penalty for disobeying an order. He even held out his hand and made us choke ourselves, just like in the movie. The wall behind the couch was scarred and dented from flying objects. There were eight-inch gashes from plates flung against it. He'd already been reported to Social Services several times for child abuse.

But he said it was his job to prepare us for war, because life was a sonuvabitch. There wasn't much he could control, but he could damn well control his sons.

"Stop crying, dammit," he'd say after beating us. "You need to toughen the hell up. Men don't whine and cry. Your mother ain't here to baby you no more."

This one time, my brother struck another kid with a stick, and his parents came to complain. My dad told them, "I'll take care of it."

They knew, just like everyone else in our neighborhood, what that meant. My dad stood in the doorway and bellowed to us, "Get your asses in here!"

We came running, squeezing past his dangling cigarette.

"When you fight, you gotta assume they are trying to kill you. Who's it gonna be—them or you?"

We stayed silent. Answering a rhetorical question could get your mouth slapped. "I asked you a question! Who is it going to be? Them? Or you? Answer me!"

"Them, Dad! Them!"

"That's right. Do not hesitate to pick up a stick or rock, or gouge an eye, or bite. You do what the fuck you gotta do to survive. Do you understand me?"

"Yes, sir."

"What?"

"YES, SIR!"

"Good. Now get up, turn around, put your hands on the couch." We heard the sound of his belt being unbuckled. "I'm only trying to help you. Someday you'll understand."

Yeah, our childhood was basically boot camp.

Boot camp for prison.

21

Lesson Learned

I was getting high long before I knew what high was. Around our house, the contact was thick! My dad was a pothead like no other, selling by the pounds and smoking by the ounces. Pot, hash, opium. Pop was in the navy, and his crew was *tight*.

In public, I always held, carried, or received because I was only nine years old. If I got caught, I didn't know any of the adults around me—"No, sir, Officer, I just found these drugs and was on my way to the po-lice."

This Saturday morning, Pop stuck his head in the room, saying, "Let's go. The park."

The park meant a morning of socializing! In other words, Pops would be smoking, drinking, and selling while I . . . washed his car. Weekends, the park was alive with chess and the music of bones. The old dogs would smoke a little, drink a little, and discuss bidness a lot. The one thing you never saw was a joint get passed. No. They never had more than two or three joints on them individually, whenever out in public. That was the rule. If you were smart.

I stalled for just a second while Pop headed to the car, then I grabbed an ounce from my stash, and we were off to the park. Once I'd washed the car, I moved to a more secluded area to get my smoke on. I'd finished one joint and was about to light another when I noticed Pops looking at me. He could see I was rolling out of a bag. I gave a nod. He nodded back.

That's when a brother strolled up. "You sellin'?"

I shook my head. "Don't know you. But you're welcome to roll one out the bag."

In less time than it takes to inhale, a pair of handcuffs snapped around my wrist. Stunned, I looked up. Next thing I knew, I was on my stomach, cuffed behind my back, and yanked back to my feet by two narcotics officers.

I risked a quick look over at Pops. He had gathered up his blanket and portable bar and was packing it away in the trunk of the car. What?! He pulled off. I almost yelled out to him as he drove past, ignoring me.

The narcs backed me up to their car. I knew they must be pleased. An ounce was a good bust. "Who'd you get this from? Just point him out and you can walk away." They waited. "All right, smart guy, let's take a ride downtown."

We'd only driven a block when I saw Pops on the side of the road by his car. The cops pulled over and got out. I did a one-eighty in the back seat trying to read their lips. What was going on?

I had been told over and over: never hold more than two joints. Never walk around with that much pot and not be doing bidness.

Turns out the cops were actually shore patrol officers, some of Pop's crew. I'd been had. Fine. No more rolling out of a bag. Lesson learned.

For four more years, I listened and learned from Pops and his crew, and then, at fourteen, I broke out on my own.

22

Better Off Dead

Man, was I ever excited. We were football fanatics, and it was the YMCA's "Take a Poor Kid to a Game Day"!

Now, I was just ten years old. Plus, I was short. But my mom didn't care; she bought all our clothes big to make sure they got plenty of wear. My orange goose-down coat was a perfect fit—for a grown *man*. It reached my shins. I looked like a walking traffic cone.

So there we were, all us Y kids, strolling through the stadium, when suddenly this white woman starts shouting, "He stole my purse! He stole my purse!"

I didn't have a clue what was going on. But outta nowhere, these five white security guards appeared. Then five more uniformed cops.

An older boy tried to run, but the cops swarmed him and pushed him into the men's room where the spectators couldn't see. They slammed the rest of us against the walls, kicked our feet apart, and frisked us. Then they forced us to our knees, hands on our heads. Over in the restroom, we could hear the older boy begging for mercy.

One cop kept patting my sleeves and pockets and asking why I had on such a big coat. When I didn't answer, he put my hands behind my back and handcuffed me.

I thought, "This is it." I figured I wouldn't live to tell about it.

They drug us below the stadium, and believe it or not, there was a jail down there. What?!

The cop walked me down a narrow corridor and asked, "You ready to talk, tough guy?"

I was too scared to speak. So he shoved me through another door into a dark labyrinth that smelled of urine. I couldn't even hear the game anymore, just dripping water. The first cage we came to, he pushed me inside and said, "One last chance, tough guy."

I just stared. Even if I'd wanted to say something, I couldn't.

He slammed the door with a smirk. "Enjoy your stay."

It was crazy. I was inside a stadium with sixty-five thousand fans who had no idea a ten-year-old child wearing an oversized winter coat was trapped in a dark hole beneath them. I figured this was where I would die.

A few minutes later, I heard a cop say, "We had to transport the older kid to Metropolitan Hospital. Not sure he's gonna make it."

Another cop answered, "I think we oughta give this tough guy some of the same medicine."

I was terrified. Nobody would know what happened to me.

Suddenly, the door opened again, and a friend's mom rushed in, asking a mile a minute, "Are you all right? Did they hurt you?"

I still couldn't talk. I just shook my head as we hurried through the hallways. We'd almost made it to the last door when the cop who'd locked me up called, "Hey, tough guy."

I turned. He aimed his index fingers and thumbs at me like a gun. I knew what he meant. In his eyes, I was better off dead.

23

Shake It Off

Our stadium was a patch of grass at the end of the apartment complex. First base: half a milk carton. Second base: a discarded potato chip bag. Third base: a bald patch where grass wouldn't grow. Home plate: the other half of the milk carton!

We played four-on-four with a broken broom handle and an old fuzzy green tennis ball.

I was ten, and it was a perfect August afternoon except I was pitching, and we were losing. But I knew we'd make a comeback soon as we got up to bat.

I was about to fire in the next pitch when two figures emerged from the woods. Grown-ups. Hot as it was, one guy was wearing a wool hat. Slung over his shoulder was a shotgun.

It wasn't the first time we'd seen guns, that's for sure, and the neighborhood had plenty of odd characters, so I was mainly just annoyed at how they just strolled through the field like they owned it. When they finally passed, I got set to pitch, but everyone else took off running.

"Hey, where y'all goin'?" I called. "I want my ups!"

Then we heard the shot. I froze. While the reverberations were still echoing off the apartment walls, the same gunman was running right past me. The wool hat now covered his face—it was a ski mask.

I sped around the corner and saw a teenage boy in a Hawaiian shirt standing by a boom box. Beside the boom box a brown paper bag was rolled around a beer. Except the young man wasn't standing; he was slinking to the ground in slow motion.

Half his head was gone.

My mouth went dry. I couldn't move. It didn't seem real. How could someone only have half a head?

A single eyeball hung out of his skull like some weird fruit. A lady was crying and screaming, "Oh God, his poor momma, his poor momma!" But I couldn't stop staring at that eyeball.

When the police came, they barely glanced at the body. An officer walked over to me and said, "You see anything?"

I couldn't speak. I guess I was in shock.

He smirked. "Man gets his head blown off in broad daylight, and no one sees anything, heh?" Then he took his baton and knocked over all the glass bottles sitting where just minutes before men had been smoking, drinking, and selling drugs.

Two attendants put on these thick, orange gloves and gathered the pieces of his brain into a baggie.

Our whole lives we'd played there on that patch of grass: tag, kickball, football.

We never played there again.

That was the end of my childhood. That was my rite of passage.

III

The Drama Was Live

(MIDDLE SCHOOL,
ELEVEN TO THIRTEEN YEARS OLD)

24

You Can Be Anything

My mother used to say, "You can be anything you want." But when words don't match up with reality, you finally stop believing.

During my sentencing, a social worker got on the stand with a stack of documents: school records, test scores, all sorts of things. He said that according to my standardized tests from fifth grade, I was literally in the top 1 percent of all students in the whole country. But somehow in sixth grade, my scores dropped into the bottom 67th percentile. He said this was alarming and absolutely unheard of. He said it was unexplainable from an academic perspective—which clearly meant that whatever the problem was, it had absolutely nothing to do with my intelligence. It was something outside of the classroom that produced this type of change. "How come someone didn't notice this?" he asked. "How come a guidance counselor didn't intervene and find out why a child in the top 1 percent of the nation drops to the bottom 67 percent in a single year?!"

I was dumbfounded. No one ever told me about my test scores. I was hearing all this for the first time. But a lot of things suddenly made sense. All the little kids from my housing project went to this pretty affluent elementary school. One of the best in the state. The teachers were hands-on. They were involved. They cared.

But for middle school, all the kids from all the housing projects in town were funneled into one school that was 85 percent black and 100 percent poor. I had seven different teachers for seven classes, so none of them really knew me. I don't think we even had guidance counselors.

I mean, I'd wanted to go to college and become an engineer. I wanted to build bridges and highways and tall buildings. I wanted to be successful and make my mom proud and be able to give her all the things she never had in life.

"You can be anything you want when you grow up." It's crazy to wake up on death row and wonder if it could ever have been true.

25

Bootleg

Grandma sold liquor and beer out of her white, shingled house. She'd moved into the house after my great-grandmother died, because the house had both plumbing and wiring. Lots of her family either lived there or stayed with her from time to time, including me.

Grandma was a bootlegger, but she also had a green thumb. She attended a vegetable garden in the backyard, and roses, tulips, and azaleas. I'd help Grandma "feed her babies" (which is how she talked about her plants) and also help her harvest the garden. Sometimes we'd pick wild blackberries for pies, poke salad for greens, and plums from the trees that lined the rocky, cratered dirt road.

Grandma also kept a steady job. After she came home from work and on weekends, she'd sell shots of liquor and beer to "friends" basically seven days a week. Family and "friends," meaning customers, would start coming over in the early evening after my grandma got home from work and in the early afternoon on the weekends. The customers would go straight to the den or kitchen, where Grandma would serve them shots of Seagram's, Smirnoff, Canadian Mist, Wild Turkey, Jack Daniels, E and J, and Crown Royal and also cans and bottles of Budweiser, Schlitz Malt Liquor Bull, and Colt 45.

Toon Loon was one of these customers. He was a lively man, but Toon didn't have any legs below the knees, so he was confined to a wheelchair that he'd speed up and down the street. Always smiling and a little—or a lot—drunk, he'd wheel himself up to us. When asked where he was headed, he'd say, "Going up to Nank's to get me a drank."

Sometimes Grandma would fry some chicken or fish on the stove, just for him. If the men weren't around, my mother, aunts, and I would help him up and down the steps of the front porch.

Toon Loon spent a lot of time at Grandma's. Probably a lot of money, too. She said he received some type of special check.

A few years earlier, my uncle and me went out walking and discovered a body on the railroad tracks. He was laid flat across the rails, as if someone had placed him exactly there for the train to run over and sever his legs. It was a sight I never forgot: on the inside of the tracks, crushed-up meat, bones, and blood encased in denim pants legs with his two shoes pointing skyward. On the outside of the tracks, the rest of his legs and torso. I was so mesmerized by the destroyed legs, I don't remember his face. I don't know how he wasn't dead.

I always wondered if Toon was the man we found, but I never worked up enough nerve to ask my uncle. And I never asked anyone else, either. We learned early that it was best not to ask too many questions.

Luxury

I never admitted to being afraid. But the first time I saw someone shot and killed close-up and also where we lived, well, after that everything changed. I made sure not to walk in front of the window that faced in that direction. If I was in the bedroom, I'd sit on the floor and play. If I was on the bed, I'd lay down flat. At night, I'd make sure the blinds were fully straightened and the curtains completely closed.

We never talked about the murder. No one ever said a thing. I mean, we still had to function. We still had to live there. There was no psychoanalysis, family counseling, or therapy. We could barely afford the necessities of life. We sure couldn't afford to break down.

I tried to suppress my fear, but I was terrified. I can still feel it now. At the time, everyone else seemed to be doing just fine. I thought if I said something, I'd be considered weak. I was a boy. At the first sign of any kind of hesitancy or tears, the rebukes would be immediate: "Stop actin' like a li'l bitch!" "What the fuck you cryin' about?" "Soft motherfucker."

It seemed like the more horrible something was, the more you were expected not to be affected. From a punch in the face to a broken bone to murder. It was just a part of life. Bullying. Danger. Death. You were expected to be hard.

What a luxury it must be to feel safe. It's something I've not known since, well, before I can remember.

Cop

In our home, the smell of cannabis was as common as Pine-Sol. My mother enjoyed the fast life—nightclubs on weekends and smoking weed every day.

Sometimes she even let me take a drag. Then she'd brag to her friends, "Look at my baby. Boy already know how to inhale. Bad ass. He gon' be somethin' else."

When I was eleven, she showed me the weed spot—an abandoned apartment building under the L train. We stepped into a space the size of a prison cell, black steel door at the end. The smell of weed was thick. We didn't even have to knock.

"What up?" said a muffled voice behind the door.

My moms answered, "Lemme get a nick."

We slid our five through this hollowed-out peep hole. A moment later, a bag of weed was shoved back. Deal done.

I guess my mother taught me how to cop because she didn't like trekking those five blocks in the cold. Maybe she figured if I was old enough to send for milk, I was old enough to send for weed.

Man of the House

I was eleven when my stepfather sat me down and said he was leaving. Stunned and betrayed, I wondered how he could just leave when we were supposed to be a family.

He explained that I was now the man of the house. It didn't seem fair. I wasn't a man. I couldn't do the things he did. I liked *The Flintstones*, Bugs Bunny, riding my bike, jumping fences, and playing football. I loved Cheetos, green Now and Laters, cookies, and chocolate milk. I wanted to cry and beg him to stay. But he wasn't asking my opinion; he was simply telling me how it was. I knew there was nothing I could say to make him stay.

He asked if I understood. I said, "Yes, sir."

Then I watched as he walked out the door.

I felt so inadequate as the "man of the house." So I stayed out at every opportunity, either at my grandma's or at my aunt's house. Any chance I got to have a sleepover, I was gone. I didn't want to be the man of the house. I was scared.

I did try, though. When my younger brother got into fights at school, they became my fights. It was more complicated with my sister. I could make a seriously mean big-brother face, but I couldn't fight girls. I wasn't sure what I was supposed to do there.

My mother was grown, but my stepdad said she needed protection, too. And I *wanted* to protect her. I adored my mother. Everything she did was for us. She never bought things for herself, but she made sure we had everything we needed. She never even raised her voice unless we got unruly. Even then, I knew it was just her loving us.

Now it was up to me to protect her. But I had an awful secret: I couldn't. I wasn't ready. I didn't know how. I didn't have the tools.

Soon, though, I would.

29

Trance

No matter how hard I tried, I couldn't hold back the tears when my father beat me. I felt so weak. He said he'd *never* let his own parents see him cry when they beat him. "I didn't give the pricks the fucking pleasure. So stop being a little fucking bitch."

Well, if that bastard could do it, so could I. I just needed to toughen up. Then, when I was about twelve, I saw a special on the Discovery Channel about some tribe of aboriginals that pushed huge knitting-needle-sized lances through their flesh. They even walked barefoot across hot coals. Somehow, the lances didn't draw blood, and the coals didn't burn them. They didn't cry out or even flinch. The tribe spoke about entering a trancelike state. From that state, they could redirect the pain, detach from it. That's what I wanted to do!

Detach. The word evoked relief. Numbness. No bleeding, no searing, no tears. No bitch-ass tears. Even a broken bone might be endured. Detach—the notion soothed me. In secret, I practiced stabbing sewing needles into my arms. Detach. When I picked up an inch of skin and shoved a needle in one side and out the other, I felt victorious for not flinching or crying. It was like that sewing needle and I had defeated my dad's lashes.

But there was a catch. Most of our dad's beatings were spontaneous. Unpredictable. And it takes time to enter a trance. So I graduated to burning myself with cigarettes and punching bricks hundreds of times. In an attempt to combat my constant fear, I became a daredevil. Anytime someone said, "I dare you" or "You scared," I did the thing.

I learned to dissociate. Not always, but I was getting better at it. I worried, though. What would I become if I could flip a switch and shut off my ability to feel? Would I be able to turn it on again?

More importantly, would I *want* to?

30

Tar Pit

At first it was just a small patch on the back of my head. Then I started pulling out my eyelashes and eyebrows. I couldn't control it. When the shrink asked in front of my parents why I was "plucking" my hair, I just felt shame and anger.

Then just as suddenly as it started, it stopped. I was in my room, alone, playing with a pocket knife and started carving on my arm. The cuts barely hurt. If anything, they felt the same as the areas where I had ripped out clumps of hair.

Mostly, it was just this huge sense of relief.

When I hit puberty, that whole onslaught of emotions, thoughts, and hormones made me extremely anxious. I started skipping classes and smoking pot, trying to soothe the frenzy of my mind.

But sometimes the frenzy in my mind got to be too much and I'd huff aerosols. Or I'd hold a lit cigarette to my arm till the skin was blistered and black. It was the only thing that helped, brought me some relief.

One time I was firing a Bic lighter to where the metal was glowing and the plastic sides caught fire. This older kid said, "If you're such a badass, hold that lighter to your arm."

I placed it against the inside of my forearm. You could hear the sizzle and smell the burning flesh.

I felt completely helpless to break out of the self-destruction. Black depression coated me like ancient tar pits. The only relief from the suffocation was getting high or harming myself.

One day when I was home alone, I loaded my dad's rifle, braced the butt between my feet, and rested the cold barrel against my forehead.

My mind kept daring me, "Do you have the balls to pull the trigger? Do you?"

I put the barrel in my mouth.

Maybe it should have occurred to me then that I was mentally ill. But it didn't.

31

Point Blank

I was only eleven, but already I knew stuff. Like, what you saw on TV wasn't real. I knew nobody in their right mind chased anyone with a gun. If somebody shot at you, you ran the other way! I knew that when a gun's drawn, ain't no witty dialogue happenin'!

It was a summer evening, but the power was out, so the neighborhood was dark. Me and my little brother were walking home from a friend's house when this boy a couple years older than us rolled up on his bike and said, "Y'all got any money?"

His voice was casual. Quiet. We shook our heads. He propped the bike against his leg. Then he pulled out a gun.

It was the first time I'd ever had a gun aimed at me point-blank. He didn't even have to ask; we just raised our hands and waited for instructions.

He started patting our pockets with one hand, holding his gun steady with the other. We were just two little boys in jeans, T-shirts, and dirty sneakers. It was pretty obvious we were poor. On our best day, we maybe had a dollar between us. I wondered if he'd shoot us for a dollar. I wondered if he'd shoot us for not having one.

I glanced at my arm. My mom had given me a watch for Christmas. A Timex. It meant a lot to me. It was a sign I was growing up. But I didn't say a word when he took it.

The boy waved the gun and said, "Start walking. Slow. And don't turn around."

Even when we heard him pedal off, we still didn't look back.

I lost more than a watch that night. When I went to bed, to school, to play, sat down to eat, I never forgot that my life could be taken from me for any reason, or for no reason at all. My life had no value. And the sooner I learned that, the better.

So I learned not to value my life. It felt empowering. If someone came to kill me, so what? The joke was on them.

After that, I never watched TV again. For us, the drama was live. And wasn't no way to change the channel.

32

Role Model

We all got role models. People who influence us. Like the neighborhood crackheads. You got your good crackheads and your bad ones. I learned a lot from watching the good crackheads that work hard, knowing they owe people. Crackheads who come home, pay their bills, then whatever's left, that's the blow.

One time my sister threatened to call Child Services. My mom walked over, grabbed the phone, and hit her upside the head with it. *Bing.*

My mom was like, "Go on and call, I bet they won't feed you like I feed you, bet they won't clothe you. I bet they won't get you what you want. But go ahead and call."

So even when my mom was mad, she still had enough love to where she was willing to keep us. She didn't have to. There was easy ways to get rid of us. Like, I was skipping a lot in middle school. And this police officer came by the house with a school official. I was shocked. They sat her down, and the school official said what he had to say, but the police just looked at her and said, "If he don't show up to school, you can pack a toothbrush. 'Cause you going away."

Afterward, I figured I was gonna get a beating, but my mom just said, "I can't make you go to school, but you're going to wish you did." I never missed another day that year. Can't say I didn't ever *skip*, but I didn't miss a whole day. Because the thought of losing her for something *I* did was too much. Like she told my sister, nobody's gonna feed me like she feeds me.

I know the sacrifices my mom made. I saw years where she had the same clothes. My little sister or brother might bitch and whine because we can't get whatever and never recognize mom don't have nothing. There was times she didn't eat. I remember seeing her choose between buying food for all us and a pack of cigarettes for herself. Well, she chose the cigarettes, 'cause she had to work, and I think she wanted to smoke while she was at work. But we still ate. And she was all right with just her pack of cigarettes.

So it made me think. My friends be like, "C'mon, let's do this," and I was like, "Nah, I can't be riding home in a police car." I know what my mom's doing for us. Now I gotta sacrifice, too.

So we all got somebody influence us. Even if it just be the good crack-heads. Even if it just be your mom.

33

Elliot MF Jones

I grew up in a housing project dead smack in middle-class affluency. It was the tolerated blemish of the West Side. Even the other projects considered us bottom rung, the busters of housing projects. We weren't hustlers or fashion trendsetters. We were "creek bamas."

Hood culture was built on three pillars: fightin', stealin', and getting drunk. Fightin' was a rite of passage and determined your position in the hood hierarchy. The better you were at fighting, the higher your status. Stealin' was our way of life. We didn't steal from one another, but outside the project, everything was for the taking. Clothes, food, money, alcohol, accessories—we stole every week. It wasn't even considered wrong; it's just what we did.

Getting drunk is how we celebrated and how we mourned. We drank to gain courage, to have fun, and to fuel the thievery and daring. Getting drunk also ended up in fights, which sometimes resulting in a reshuffling of the hood hierarchy.

The top of the hood pyramid was Elliot Jones. He was the meanest, baddest mofo I ever seen in my life! He didn't fear anyone. Including cops. He was the Top Dog, and his reputation extended throughout the city. He was the leader of a crew called the Four Horsemen, and they were all bodybuilders. But Elliot "Muthafuckin'" Jones, which is how we referred to him, was a Monster! He had a bench set up outside with barbells and dumbbells, and all he did all day was lift weights, drink, and terrorize anyone who crossed his path.

I learned from watching him that respect was earned through violence and maintained by more. You had to be cold, brutal, with zero tolerance. I was both terrified and in awe of him. I wanted the respect he commanded. I wanted people to tremble when they heard my name. I wanted men to be afraid to utter a bad opinion of me. I wanted to be like Elliot MF Jones because everybody was afraid of him! *Including* the boys who bullied me.

Whenever I saw those boys squirm in his presence, I felt a deep satisfaction. Particularly one of the boys, who called me pussy boy and halfbreed. I hated him with all my heart. When they cowered in Elliot's presence, it made me realize that deep down they were just like me, afraid. But Elliot, he wasn't afraid of nobody! He would slap one guy because he didn't like his T-shirt, call another over for a sip of wine and then knock him cold for drinking too much.

Anytime the cops came to arrest him, they called him "Mr. Jones" and "sir" and asked if he would mind coming downtown with them. They were afraid of him 'cause he had knocked out some of them before. He'd even been shot. But what could a bullet do to Elliot Jones?

I was much too young to be worthy of anything more than a "What the fuck you lookin' at, boy?" from Elliot MF Jones, at which I took off running. I was just a curly-headed mixed boy at the bottom of the hood hierarchy. But occasionally I received a punch in the chest or a threat that he would beat my ass if I didn't go all the way with some girl he claimed had a crush on me. Then I would fantasize about what it would be like to be Elliot Jones. How I would love to call all my tormentors one by one as they crossed my path.

"Hey, you, come here." (*Smack, smack.*) "Get your bitch ass in the house, pussy boy." And "What the fuck you lookin' at, boy?" (*Wham!*)

That's who I looked up to. That's who I wanted to be. The Top Dog. Elliot Muthafuckin' Jones!

34

Suspension of Disbelief

Junior High.

It was the worst of times mainly due to our principal. Basically, this man spent the last two years of junior high proving how Black was NOT Beautiful. Proving it with four suspensions I didn't deserve.

I was standing with a bunch of white guys. One had a ponytail almost to his ass, and another had his hair in pigtails. But the principal grabbed me, saying, "What have you done to your hair?"

"It's cornrows," I said.

"You look like a girl," he taunted.

Girl? Man, I was the only dude in the seventh grade with a mustache.

"You can't come to my school looking like that."

Suspended.

Another time he came up to me and asked why I was wearing a blouse.

"It's a dashiki," I explained.

"You look like a girl."

Suspended.

Now, I admit the third suspension was kind of my fault. I admitted to pulling the fire alarm. The principal was threatening to cancel field day if someone didn't confess. So I played the hero. My track coach told him that I was in the high-jump pit and couldn't have done it. But our principal was perfectly happy to sacrifice a black kid, even if he knew it wasn't true.

My last suspension was actually at the graduation dance. Not only was the DJ playing "Old Black Joe," some students were laughing and singing along. "Gone are the days when my heart was young and gay, / Gone are my friends from the cotton fields away. . . ." Man, are you kidding me? That California school was lucky there were only seven black students. All we could do was hang our heads, boiling in anger and shame.

So maybe I deserved that fourth suspension. 'Cause when the DJ wasn't looking, I switched the track to Sly Stone's "Don't Call Me Nigger, Whitey."

If the principal had just been listening, he'd've heard the next line: "Don't call me whitey, nigger." That's all I wanted. Equality.

But he wasn't listening. Ever.

IV

From Bad to Worse

(FOURTEEN YEARS OLD TO ARREST)

A Wrap

As a teen, you just have very limited vision. You can't see very far into the future. I was a few months into ninth grade when our assistant principal called me to the office. She said, "Every tardy is an absence."

I'm like, "All right." Then I think, "But I ain't never been to first period. I don't even know what that teacher look like."

She says again, "Do you understand what I'm telling you?"

I'm like, "Not really."

She goes, "Late arrivals are unacceptable. Three tardies equals one absence, and nine absences is the limit."

I must have just been staring at her, 'cause then she says, "You can't miss more than nine days in a semester. You've already missed so many that even if you come to school every day and make straight A's, you still won't pass."

I thought she was joking. It was still the beginning of the year. I was like, "So you're telling me I can go clean out my locker?"

She says, "Yeah," like she was relieved I finally understood.

So I just walked out. I was halfway home, thinking, "My momma's going to kill me." She tried to call up there to see if there was a way to work something out, but they told her there was nothing she could do.

School had just started. So it was a whole year on my own. After that year, my life was a wrap.

JD

My first year of high school, our class was approximately 65 to 70 percent black. My school didn't teach black history, so the alternative was for me to join the Black Culture Club. It was headed by the school's guidance counselor. Voluntarily coming to school at 7:00 a.m. was a pain in the ass, but worth the hemorrhoid. This counselor viewed us as future voters and activists, so he taught us how to covertly organize parties at the school as a means of catching the ears of other future voters.

That's where I met another freshman, JD. Together, we planned to go to a school party and hand out pamphlets with information ranging from police brutality to sexually transmitted diseases. When we entered the dark embrace of the school's gym, I was feeling "fresh to death" in a crisp pair of high-top, black-and-white, shell-toe Adidas and my cousin's black Gucci frames. We took separate routes, but I kept JD in my sights.

He had a magnetic personality that made people want to listen to him. He was a born community activist. He genuinely cared about people and stood up for those afraid to stand up for themselves. Who knows what could have been had I matched JD's intensity for activism? But the chicks and the almighty dollar were my motivations. I was no longer the weak kid that cried at the sight of police beating and humiliating black people. I had grown out of that. I was now a smart, good-looking teenager that loved girls and hated being broke.

JD became my best friend. I didn't see him over the Christmas break, but we talked a few times over the phone. "We ain't promised to survive these streets," he reminded me. "Some of us ain't gonna see graduation, man. We gotta save some lives."

Before he could go any deeper, I rushed him off the phone. I was just too damn selfish.

That winter, JD was stabbed with a steak knife by another kid our age. Police claimed the altercation stemmed from a snowball fight. I can still see JD's face in the newspaper. His blood left a trail in the snow where family members drug his lifeless body to the house.

Sitting at the funeral, I felt only shame. Why him and not me? His face was swollen, and his mouth looked as if he was trying to say something. "Some of us ain't gonna see graduation, man."

I touched his right hand. It lay over his heart as if he was still feeling the pain there. "We gotta save some lives."

37

When We Were Young

I guess the little kid was lost in thought. At the Youth Detention Center, we sometimes stood for hours, waiting to get count right. Not this time. When the kid in the eleven spot said, "Twelve," the staffer shouted, "Hold the fuck up!"

He stomped over, grabbed the kid's jumpsuit, and screamed into his face, "Your goddamn number is eleven! Eleven! Count again!"

We got all the way to twenty-three. Then silence.

The staffer started yelling again. "Why the hell were you looking out the window? Is it because your mammy smoked crack while you festered in her womb? Or are you a fucking retard?!"

The kid mouthed off and that was all the staffer needed. He grabbed a fistful of the boy's brown hair, yanked him closer, kneed him in the stomach, and flipped the kid to the floor. Then he pressed his knee into the kid's back and pulled the alarm for backup.

The extra guards who swarmed in seemed disappointed to find the boy already subdued. They zip-tied the kid's hands behind his back, attached his feet, and lifted him like a suitcase.

When the kid cried out, one of the guards kicked him in the ribs and said, "Shut up! You need yourself some behavior modification." Aka Intensive Care.

In Intensive, they stripped you naked, turned the AC on high, and shoved you into a cell with a hole in the floor for a toilet. No light. At some point, they'd give you a pair of skivvies and a thin mat. If you fought, pissed off the staff, or harmed yourself, you could spend weeks in there, twenty-three hours a day in the dark.

The Hole was a scary place where food was sparse and clothing a privilege. There was nothing to read. No TV or music. Talking was forbidden, so when we could, we whispered to each other between the cracks under the door. I made it through long days and even longer nights in that hell by pacing, counting cinder blocks, singing half-remembered songs, and clinging to the thought that it wouldn't last forever, even if it felt that way.

The hardest part of doing the time was hearing the kids who acted up get beaten by adults who were supposed to be our legal guardians and caretakers. Kids who tried to escape the Youth Detention Center landed in the hospital.

If they were lucky.

One time, I got in trouble for talking. As punishment, I had to write, *I am a sick man* one thousand times before I could eat. The staff said the sooner I realized I had a problem, the better. *I am a sick man.* One. *I am a sick man.* Two.

38

Stinging Bee

School was a serious impediment to my fourteen-year-old love life. So I decided to cut class to go visit my girl's school across town.

I'm hanging in her gym, watching some hoops, when a school police officer decides he's gonna earn his paycheck and hauls me up to the office for trespassing.

So, there I am in the principal's office, weighing my options: go to jail or call my mom? Seriously, I couldn't decide which was worse. I'm a minor—they lock me up, I ain't going to be down there too long. And my mom, well, she was what you call real heavy-handed.

My aunts used to tell stories about how my mom would protect her sisters, even if it meant fighting boys. She didn't play no games when it came to men trying to be aggressively physical in a degrading manner. She was known to fight, and trust me, she packed a powerful punch. The boys in the neighborhood started calling her "Stinging Bee" because she'd punch people in the mouth.

As a mom, she was one of those freestyle-type disciplinarians, you feel me? A belt was fine if it was handy; otherwise, she improvised. One minute, you're playing with your Hot Wheels track, and the next minute, that track is tracking *you*!

But I also had trust issues with the police. I figured I might never make it *to* the police station. So I give the principal my mom's phone number.

I'm sitting in the chair, the principal and the two police standing beside me, when the receptionist opens the office door and there's my mom wheeling that corner with this look on her face. All I see is her fist. Hits me with a two piece and knocks me out in the chair.

When I finally gather myself together, the first thing I hear is the police say to the principal, "Looks like everything's taken care of here. We'll just be on our way."

Stinging Bee. She packed a powerful punch, all right.

39

Hands On

Drugs and violence seemed commonplace and normal until I'd go to a friend's house and see how different they were living. Their house was peaceful, clean, good-smelling. Mine was hectic, with dirty clothes everywhere, and always smelling like some kind of drug smoke.

One night my stepfather took a swig of tea and told my mother it was too sweet. When she put the glass to her mouth to taste it, he smashed the glass against her face, chipping two teeth. Then he started hitting her.

I ran across the street to a neighbor's house and asked them to call the cops. But like always, my mom told the cops nothing was the matter. So the cops left, and I got my ass beat by my mom for trying to help her.

When I asked why, she said, "I don't need any help. Don't ever do that again."

After every fight, they'd reconcile. I just didn't get it. I hated living in all that chaos. I hated watching my mom get beat. I never understood why she put us through that, year after year.

Then one day she overslept. I heard my stepdad hit the alarm hard to cut it off and yell, "You forgot to get the damn kids up for school." He stomped into the kitchen. A few minutes later I hear, "Bitch, get your ass up" and a scream. He had thrown a pot of hot water on her.

The last time I found my mother crumpled on the floor, I grabbed my stepdad, threw him up against the wall, and punched him as hard as

I could in the jaw. There was a loud *pop* that said it all: I was no longer a boy, and I would not stand by and watch this man beat my mom. I was fourteen years old and a football player. He was just some skinny crackhead who hit women.

I looked him in the eyes and said, "Don't you ever hurt my mom again." Then I went to get my sister ready for school.

And he never did.

40

On My Own

The one person in the world I sort of trusted was my mom. And then, one day in October, I learned she was addicted to the crack she sold. Man! My disappointment was unbearable. She'd violated a cardinal rule of the game: "Don't get high on your own supply."

We argued, and I smashed everything of value in the apartment. I wanted to make it impossible for her to ever buy more crack. Truthfully, I think I assaulted the appliances to keep from assaulting her.

She phoned my school. The social worker and a counselor called me into the office. I didn't say much. I was embarrassed. My mom claimed we'd argued because I had drugs on me. She neglected to mention the small detail about her smoking crack.

The counselor confiscated my bag of weed. I couldn't believe my mother had snitched on me. And lied!

I'd forgotten my keys, so when I got home, I knocked and called through the door.

Nothing. My mom refused to let me into my own home. I went ballistic, banging and kicking the door. Finally, a housing cop showed up.

My mother told him I had drugs on me and that's why she wouldn't let me in. I felt like I'd been kicked in the gut. She'd sold me out to a cop?! I stared at her in disbelief, my whole world shattered. The one person I thought I could trust had betrayed me. I was speechless.

There was nothing for the housing cop to find. He let me go. I stepped into the night. I was fifteen, homeless, and on my own.

I had been afraid my whole life, but now was no time to show it. I did whatever was necessary to survive. I was still a child, but I knew from the womb that fear was a sign of weakness. The world was hard and cruel. You eat or are eaten. I became a beast lest I become a meal.

My mother and I didn't speak again until I was twenty-one.

41

Ain't Got No Name

The old guys on the corner used to say, "A bullet ain't got no name," meaning a bullet could hit, hurt, or kill anyone. Even the small guns were lethal. And they all made the most god-awful sound. Anytime I saw a gun, I knew something was about to go down. Where we lived, it wasn't the animals that were hunted; it was the people.

We'd recently moved out of the city, but where we lived everyone was poor, just like the last place we'd moved from, and the place before that. My mom worked hard all her life. All she ever wanted was for us to be safe, but we could only afford to live in places that weren't.

Soon after we moved into the apartment, there was an attempted break-in. My mom and sister told me how scared they'd been. They slept in the same bed, and my mom slept with a knife under her pillow. So the next weekend, my brother and I stayed home.

Late one night, there was a knock on the door. It was Fat Mike. We were thrilled to see a friendly face. We showed him around the new apartment and made him some fried hot dogs. He told us he'd heard about the break-in.

As he was leaving, he placed a gun in my hand. "Protect your mother and sister."

The gun was small, a .25-caliber automatic. It fit inside the palm of my hand but had a weight like a thud, a dead weight. Inside our apartment that smelled of air freshener and hot dogs, the black and steel was cold to the touch. The gun was a gift, but it didn't feel like one.

The first thing we did was hide it. I'd always heard it was better to have a gun and not need it than to need one and not have it. But even hidden, the gun was still present in my brother's and my thoughts; we were always conscious of where it was. We were afraid of our sister finding it, of us carrying it and being stopped by the police. Worse, I was afraid I might have to use it.

I'd seen people shot before. Some were killed right there on the spot, some survived, and others I wasn't sure. I swore to myself that I would not be anybody's victim, if I could help it. But the stakes for pulling that trigger seemed awfully high.

I was the oldest and had a responsibility to protect my mom and my younger siblings. In a world so vast, they were all I had. I didn't want to shoot anyone, I didn't want to take a life, but my family *was* my life, and if anyone posed a threat to them, well, I was the man of the house.

It was a miserable situation. I understood why kids in that area would join a gang; kids do dumb stuff all the time. But the grown-ups were just as bad. My mom basically just barricaded herself inside the apartment. When my sister went to school, the other kids picked fights with her. We taught her how to defend herself.

But when one of the boys jumped her, my brother and I got involved. Sometimes all a powder keg needs to explode is that one spark that hits just right. I used the gun.

The act didn't make me feel heroic or proud, but I wasn't ashamed. There was no music playing in the background, just a teenage boy shot in the chest and people screaming and running. We ran as well; we were scared, too. Amid all the chaos and running, we threw the gun away. I was mad at myself for running; it's what I'd done my whole life.

We went to a pay phone and called home. My mother was frantic. The police were already there. I turned myself in.

I have no idea who found that gun. But I'm pretty sure that whatever their story, it didn't have a happy ending. Not if it involved a gun.

42

Slap in the Face

I was the smart kid from the hood. At sixteen, I was on course to graduate high school early. I had serious plans to go to college. The streets weren't gonna claim me. I would defy the odds and prove everyone wrong. I was attending the High School of Graphic Arts and Communication. My goal was to become a graphic artist.

Then I got expelled.

Me and this kid were slap-boxing in the stairwell. Somewhere in all the slapping, the boy got mad and grabbed me. Now, I was always a skinny dude, so this didn't go so well for me. The kid pulled me into a choke hold, and I couldn't get him off me.

It was turning into a really bad situation, but like most kids from the ghettos, I carried a weapon for protection. Before things could go from bad to worse, I whipped out my butterfly knife. The kid ran off.

It never even crossed my mind the kid would tell. Even a kinder-gartener knew snitching was wrong. But he did. A school police guard pulled me out of class and took me to the dean's office. They searched me and found the knife.

My grades were good. I'd never missed a day of school. I was foreman of my shop class. But I lived in the hood, and only a fool didn't carry protection. None of this was taken into consideration. I was expelled and sent to a school for "automotive studies."

Fuck it, I thought. Who was I to aspire to go to college? I was a young black male in America. I was supposed to drop out, go to prison, or die young. My father'd been in prison most of my life. Hell, my grandparents were in prison for selling drugs. My mother sold. Who was I kidding?

Bold as hell, I went home and told my mother I was going to sell weed. I wish I knew what she was thinking when she stared at me a moment before simply saying, "Be careful."

43

Doing My Job

I hadn't lived with my mom in a long time. We'd had a kind of on-off relationship, mostly because of her drug use, and neglect, and the fact that she married a man that beat her. The list goes on.

But she had broken free of her toxic marriage and her drug use. Now she had a new man with three kids of his own. Things were surprisingly good. I came home and, for the first time, felt like I was with a real family. There was just was one thing missing. My little sister.

My sister's father wouldn't allow her to leave his place. But he wasn't taking care of her at all. He left her, a nine-year-old, to cook for herself (when there was food in the house), to clean herself, and to get herself up and ready for school. Why? Because he was out-of-his-mind high.

The school principal had called my mom saying that my sister was demonstrating poor hygiene: wearing the same clothes three days in a row and smelling like she hadn't had a bath in days.

I could feel my anger rising. As calmly as I could, I asked my mom's boyfriend, "You mind if I borrow your truck for about thirty minutes?"

My mom asked, "Where you going, baby?"

"To get my sister," I said.

As I drove, I was thinking of all the stuff I was gonna do to my stepdad for treating my sister like this. I pulled up in the driveway, and when my sister saw who it was, she came tearing over to hug me.

My stepdad shrank back to the porch, eyes wide, rubbing his hands together, with a hitch in his step. I knew he was high right then. I'd been around it too many times not to recognize the signs. And suddenly all the stuff I was thinking of doing to him just turned to pity.

"Brother, what you doing here?" my sister asked.

"I come to take you to mama. Now, go get some clothes and your school stuff."

She ran back in the house and gathered a very few things.

"Where's she going?" my stepdad asked me.

I just said, "To my mama."

There was a brief stare down, then he shrugged, "All right."

After that day, my sister never seen her father again. My mom always gave her the option, but I guess she was just too scarred.

Both my mom and my sister have thanked me for going to get her that day. My sister went from missing days at school and failing to getting on the A/B honor roll and even getting awards on award day. Considering where she came from, she's done pretty good for herself.

White Devil

I don't know when it began, her affair with that white devil. Maybe it was a pipe, a stem, or crushed up in a cigarette and turned into smoke. It invaded her like a ghost, penetrated her mind, seeped into the soft tissue of her heart, and kicked down the door to her soul.

She did it because she was hurt. Her daddy touched her in a way that daddies aren't supposed to touch their little girls. She was only nine. But he continued to touch her. Until it was more than touching. He made her keep it a secret. Until one day four years later when her mother walked in.

Her mother kicked her out. I found her four years later with scars on her wrists and wounds much deeper than that. I was just a boy myself; how could I heal such a broken soul? Still I gave her all I had, thinking my love could protect her from the pain in her heart.

But she had already found her comfort in crack. She did it in silence, without my knowledge. But that devil in the fire killed everything inside her that wasn't already dead, including my son.

Don't do it! I wish I could've yelled that before the devil ever possessed her soul. But how many words does it take to actually change the course of a life? Would yelling "Don't do it" at her daddy have changed his actions? Or yelling "Don't do it" to whoever corrupted him?

Or would all the "Don't do its" in the world not have mattered in the end?

Voices in the Dark

The park wasn't a place to walk alone at night. It was divided by a slow-moving creek with a thin metal bridge connecting the two halves. A concrete pathway wound under a heavy canopy of trees. Except for the crickets and frogs, you could've been walking down a pitch-black hallway.

It was four of us: me; my cousin; an old friend, Silo; and Miguel. In front of us, Silo and Miguel were nothing but silhouettes.

My longtime friend Silo turned and passed me a blunt, then he and Miguel kept walking. I took a hit and handed it sideways to my cousin. He took a long pull, and in the orange glow, I saw he was holding a gun. He leaned toward me and hissed, "If I shoot this motherfucker, will you help me dump his body in the creek?"

Bam! My high was *gone*.

See, about three weeks earlier, my cousin and my old friend Silo showed up at my house on the same day, both fresh from Queens, New York. Everything was cool till they discovered they were from opposing hoods. Then my room became a boxing ring.

My mother busted in, "If you want to act like niggas, get outta my house."

Outside, in the parking lot, I'm like, "How'd I just get kicked out of my own house for *y'all* fightin'?" But they went at it again. Silo pulled an ice pick. We're like, "Eighty-six the ice pick or we'll do it for you," so he put it away and went back to fighting fair.

About then my mother stomped outside, yelling for us to leave the apartment complex. I barely managed a step before she hollered, "Where do you think you're going? Get in this house."

Yes, ma'am.

Afterward, my friend Silo skipped school for a week to let the swelling go down. I figured the whole mess was over.

Until now. My cousin asked again, "Well? You with me?"

Before he could do anything, I snatched the blunt and passed it forward to Miguel with a "Y'all smoke the rest."

Then I pulled my cousin back. "I thought it was dead."

My cousin said, "That dude got me kicked out of my auntie's house. And your mom still ain't invited me back. That shit ain't dead."

I could tell his mind was made up. Damn. I scrambled to think of some way to divert him. I knew he liked Miguel. "Listen, ain't no way Miguel will keep quiet. He'll crack in a day."

My cousin wavered. "Well . . ."

I was afraid he might decide to get rid of Miguel, too. So quickly I added, "Plus, his mama just watched us all leave together. She gonna know you at least saw something."

By this time Silo had started getting suspicious. He called back, "Y'all all right?"

There was a long pause.

Then my cousin said, "Yeah, thought I saw something." And put the gun away.

I saved two lives that night. And neither of 'em ever knew.

46

Finally

The last time my father tried to beat me, I was seventeen.

My brother and I had just finished working out with our weights when our dad burst into the room in a rage and came after my brother swinging. He punched my brother in the stomach, and it was on. The bench toppled, bars and plates clattered, all of us were yelling.

Finally, my brother pinned our father against a wall, screaming for him to calm down. He wouldn't. Dad was frothing in fury, his face red with exertion.

I stood there crying in frustration, shaking, keening. I heard buzzing in my ears as blood flooded my brain. Like always, I didn't know when I had enough, until I did. I snapped.

Without thinking, I snatched up a five-pound, foot-long chrome bar, stepped forward, and pinned one of our dad's arms to the wall while my brother did the same. Except for our ragged breathing, it was quiet.

"This stops today, right now! Do you hear me?!" I screamed so hard, white flecks of foam specked his grizzled cheek. "We are your SONS, not your personal fucking punch bags. Your SONS. We love you, but we will fucking kill you; we will beat you to death back here if you don't stop trying to hurt us!"

I was totally prepared to slam the bar I held onto his head. The tension in the air and in my muscles felt electric.

Our dad quit struggling and looked us both in the eyes. Tears brimmed up in his as he choked out a single sentence.

"Finally . . . my boys have become MEN."

47

Crossing Over

I made my crossover when I was twelve years old.

We were living in a housing project where well-behaved, bright children got sucked into the quicksand of negativity. My friends and I were poor, and we got paid money, *real* money, and clothes, and food to hold the drug dealers' packages and guns. When Five-O came on the block, we kids just rode off on our bicycles with whatever we were holding. The police didn't bother the kids, and that left the drug dealers safe during shakedowns.

We soon graduated from just holding packages to hunting down customers who "jumped the fence," meaning they dodged paying the dealers what they owed them. At first, we just tracked them down like an adolescent pack of wolves. Then we progressed to "making 'em dance"— shooting them in the feet and ass with automatic pistols.

Even as a kid, I realized that once you cross over from civilian to combatant, it's almost impossible to cross back. I went to school during the day and participated in crime at night. When I was a junior in high school, I was the track team's star athlete. I even assisted in coaching teammates in the long and triple jumps. Then, after school, I sold crack cocaine and illegal guns.

One Friday night, I was riding around as usual with my cousins and a few other friends. I kept imploring my cousin to take me home. The following day was a highly anticipated track meet at the university. My coach had told me there would be recruiters watching me for a scholarship. This was a great opportunity for me and my family. I needed to be home early so I could get some good rest.

But my cousin had other ideas. He wanted to stop at the carnival at the local mall first. Soon after we arrived at the carnival, we saw another group of guys. I knew one of the guys had a beef with my cousin about a girl, so both groups watched each other warily. We knew they had at least one gun. Maybe more. My cousin had a single gun under his shirt. Finally, the other guys left, and the tension dissipated.

I kept insisting my cousin take me home, and finally he relented. That's when I noticed the other group's white car edging our way across the parking lot.

"They're about to roll on us!" I yelled, then dipped behind some cars.

They pulled their car behind ours, blocking us in.

My cousin yelled to the other guy, "Let that shit go, man. I don't mess with yo girl no more."

I chimed in, "Let it go, man. Let that shit go."

"I ain't letting it go." The guy opened his door and stepped out, pistol in hand.

I was a sprinter. I could cover a lot of turf in a few seconds. I ran to the driver's side of our car. As I passed my cousin, he lifted his shirt, showing his gun. I grabbed and cocked the gun as I whirled to face our pursuer. He was just rounding the rear of our car with his pistol drawn.

POP! I shot him at point-blank range. As he fell, I shot three more times. I didn't need to, but in combat, actions are pure reflex. He lay on the pavement.

"Run! The other nigga got a gun!" my cousin yelled. As I jumped into the car, he opened fire on us, and I returned fire, stitching up his arm and into his shoulder.

It wasn't until then I realized I'd been shot. Twice. Just then, two girl-friends drove by and called the paramedics. When the police arrived, I gave them the gun.

The next day, when two detectives arrived at our home, I was prepared to go to jail. To my surprise, they said the DA had interviewed witnesses and determined it was justifiable homicide. Case closed.

But it wasn't closed with me. I hated what happened. The guy I killed was twenty years old. Why was he dead and not me?

My family and friends at home, school, and around the community treated me like a war hero awarded the Medal of Honor. But not my dad. "Son, you killed that boy," he said somberly as he twisted a wrench inside an engine of a car. He wasn't proud of what I'd done; he didn't pat me on the back like everyone else.

He had my back as always, but we weren't going to celebrate death.

V

Given the Circumstances

(JAIL TO TRIAL AND SENTENCING)

48

A Kind of Peace

I don't think either of my parents had their high school diplomas or GEDs. I remember being thirteen and wondering how I was gonna make it through high school. Because by the time I turned fourteen years old, my life had been practically an *entire* life of violence, abuse of all kinds, and also neglect. So I didn't see even making it to high school.

But I sort of made it by mistake. Not being able to write. Not being able to read much. The behavior problems I had—not eating properly, not resting properly, having to deal with so many emotions, with family, with living in the neighborhood I lived in—all that just didn't provide any time for me to receive a good education.

The day I was arrested, we were most likely going off to smoke and sort of hang out, basically do the things we always did. With no thought at all to having committed a crime. At the time, we didn't realize anybody had died. And we also didn't realize the severity of death. In my mind, he was all right, just not around. We didn't know what happened to him. We had no realization what *could* happen.

That morning, I woke up and wanted to see my friend, so first thing I did was walk over there. His uncle came to the door and said, "What have you guys done? The police are looking for you. They're coming to get you."

I was confused. It didn't dawn on me that a person had died. All I knew was, on that particular night, we were taking up for ourselves. We weren't gonna be bullied anymore, and I finally had a friend who was gonna be there *with* me and be there *for* me.

As for the police, in my neighborhood we didn't have good feelings about the police. So when I heard they were coming to get me, I ran. All day, just running around. I knew they were looking for me, but I had no history with the judicial system, besides what others in my neighborhood said.

By the end of that night, the police had contacted my mother. I don't know what they told her, but she decided to turn me in.

So she called me. And she kept me on the phone long enough that the police could come and arrest me, which is testament to our relationship. I think, at this point, my mother was feeling like she couldn't control me. Couldn't take care of me, which I knew, because she never *had*. For as long as I could remember, it had been my job to take care of myself.

It was a betrayal. A real betrayal. First of all, it was a betrayal in our community, and second of all, in our relationship. She was my first teacher, and she had always said we had no business with the police. They don't come into our neighborhoods, they don't help us, they don't do anything for us but arrest us, incarcerate us, shoot us, and kill us. So we had no business with the police. We were raised this way. This is how our communities react to the presence of the police.

When she turned me in, she was doing two things: getting rid of a bad kid that she couldn't take care of or control, and finally relieving herself of the problem of having a child that she never wanted in the first place. So I felt betrayed, I felt hurt by it. But that doesn't mean I don't love my mother; I do. She's all that I have.

When I was arrested, it was a shock. I was told what to say. I was told what to do. I didn't get to speak hardly anything for myself. I understand now they coerced me. But at the time, I didn't really know what was happening. I just wanted for it to be over so I could sleep. To try and get away from these intense feelings.

It was a harsh change. The mind resists, the heart resists. I was still in the very first stages of puberty, so my emotions and my mind were all in turmoil, they were all over everywhere. It was hard for me to understand and to cope with that new environment, to cope with being fourteen years old and sentenced to die in prison.

But in a lot of ways, there was more opportunity in that environment than I'd had previously. I didn't look healthy before. I was so small for my age; I was late in puberty. From the time of my arrest to the time I went to trial, I actually gained forty or fifty pounds. For the first time in my life, I was eating regularly. For the first time, resting regularly. I was bathing. I wasn't doing drugs; I wasn't smoking weed every day or cigarettes. I wasn't staying up all night.

So after I got arrested, I started to have characteristics of a healthy young fourteen-year-old. In prison, my life was a lot less chaotic, a lot more regular. There was a kind of peace to being there.

49

Seeing the Light

The place looked like any old high-rise apartment. Till you noticed the razor wire and gun towers. The boys locked up there were as young as twelve. They were in for anything from shoplifting to arson or murder. Didn't matter. The treatment was the same.

Kids waiting for trial who were deemed high risk or high profile were isolated on the thirteenth floor. We were locked in a solitary cell with no toilet and no running water for twenty-three hours a day. There was only one restroom for the twenty-four kids. So any empty soda bottles, milk cartons, or Styrofoam cups, we kept.

As soon as I arrived at the facility, this immense guard strip-searched me, gave me a yellow jumpsuit, then handcuffed me behind the back and pushed me into a dayroom. A group of kids were sitting in plastic chairs.

"Go to your cells!" snapped another stocky guard and then spat into a dented soda bottle. Through the haze of psych meds, I wondered what to expect.

The kids in their yellow jumpsuits scattered down the hallway and into their cells, doors clicking behind them.

The guard, who had a wide, thin mouth, bulging throat, and no neck and seemed more toad than man, motioned for the other guard. A tall, lanky man, he snatched the limp bag of my belongings and dumped them on the floor. Then the toad guard said, "Take his cuffs off."

I knew the setup. You get mad over the way they treat your property, and they beat the crap out of you. I stayed silent, rubbing my sore wrists.

Then the toad guard smiled. "What you in for, boy?"

The heavy doses of meds numbed and calmed me, but the question still made me shudder. I could remember nothing of the heinous murder I was charged with, and even that half thought seemed to edge my mind toward madness.

It was none of their damn business, so I said, "Stealing cars and selling drugs."

The tall guard spat again and said, "You a real smart sum-bitch, ain't you? We know how come you're here. Your shit's been all over the news, boy."

I'd spent what seemed like a lifetime on the street, but I'd never been much of a troublemaker. So I was unprepared for what came next. The toad guard pushed me into the nearest empty cell, slammed me against the wall, and backhanded me. He whipped out his baton and with a smooth motion jammed it under my chin, pressing hard as my arms flailed.

"I hate punks like you. You think killin's fun? I'll show you fun!"

He pressed harder. I choked and gagged. When I tried to push him away, the tall guard punched his baton into my ribs. One, two, three times. Everything started going dark. The only thing holding me against the wall was the baton in the toad guard's two-fisted grip. Then the tall guard jammed his into me a fourth time, and I went unconscious.

They kicked me awake, laughing as I sobbed in air. My face was covered in tears and snot and blood.

The guard spat on the floor and warned me, "We hear a peep out of you, we'll come back and string you up. Understand? Ain't nobody gon' care. All we say is we come back and found you hanging." He stared at me. "You understand me, boy? We straight?"

They slammed the cell door behind them.

I have no idea how long I lay curled there on the floor, heart hammering and face bleeding. Everything I had in the world—four letters, a tube of toothpaste, a toothbrush, and a small pencil—was stamped with their boot prints.

Then I saw the light. I stared at that bare light bulb and thought about breaking the glass and using a piece to cut my throat. It was the only object in my tiny world that gave me any power over the terror, isolation, and helplessness I now felt.

That light bulb was the only hope I had.

50

Boy

It was a beautiful warm summer morning.
Walking to my job assignment at the canteen warehouse,
I was full of energy and in great spirits.
I nodded at my supervising officers,
sipping coffee from their personalized mugs,
they barely acknowledged my presence.
I said I was going to organize some of the clutter in the hallway.
Tanks of carbonated water used for refilling fountain drinks
impeded the way, making it difficult to maneuver and wheel
the hand trolley through the narrow halls.
After relocating the metal tanks to a better location,
the head supervisor walked into the warehouse
in his usually upbeat manner,
hands in his pockets and a vibrant hum
that seemed to radiate from his body.
His eyes, like a hawk, scanned my work with a smile.
He then sauntered into his office and returned with two subordinates.
"Who moved the tanks from the hallway?"
the head supervisor asked while looking at me
with a seemingly accusatory smile.
"I did," I said, feeling a bit self-conscious,
fearing he was implying that something might be amiss.

His eyes lit up like he had caught a thief.
"Put them back," he said, rising up on his toes,
then snapping his heels onto the hardwood floor.
He looped his thumbs through his belt loops
in a posture of superiority and condescension.
"I just moved them over here . . ." I pointed,
hoping he would see that it was a better place.
"It's hard to maneuver the hand trolley—"
He cut me off.
"You don't move nothing in here
unless you ask me first.
Do you understand me, boy?
I'm the boss in here.
Now put them back where you found them."
Gone was the mask of friendly kindness.
He had called me "boy."
The lines had been drawn.
I was no longer just an inmate,
and he wasn't just an officer in a warehouse anymore.
He was reminding me of my "real" place:
it was white against black
and I suddenly felt intimidated,
outnumbered, and afraid.
I looked away from his eyes.
His two subordinates stood like henchmen on either side of him
like they were ready to pounce, set me up, or fabricate some lie
to justify whatever they intended to do.
Just leave, I thought, as my heart began to beat rapidly.
I turned the knob on the door and began to pull it open.
A hand pushed it closed in opposition.
"Where do you think you're going?"
I looked back into menacing eyes in the once friendly face.
"I'm going back to the camp," I said, turning away.
"You ain't going nowhere, nigger!"
Whoosh! It knocked the wind out of me.
My heart shriveled with shame.
Until *that* moment when he uttered *that* word,

a part of me would've still been able to deny
that any of this was real. But now . . .
I met his gaze for a final time, and in that moment
we saw one another, unmasked, for the first time.
He stumbled back as if shocked and moved out of my way.
I turned the knob. The warm summer sun kissed my cheeks
as the tears spilled
heavily down my face.

51

The Quiet Room

It should have been oil-tanker obvious, perched on the horizon of my future, but I was a particularly dense teenager. First, I didn't think I was *really* crazy. Sure, there were times I felt the need to walk in front of a speeding semi or flay the skin from my body, but times were hard, and these seemed like natural responses to me. Second, even though I was in a hospital wing for the mentally disturbed, because I was indeed mentally disturbed, I still felt like the same old me. There was just a lot of bullshit going on in my life that millions of people deal with all the time. I knew dealing should come as naturally as the crap, but it didn't, and that was the problem. Third, something about being in an institutional setting with all the restrictions just seemed to call out my wild side.

My mom had just visited. This is how I found myself in the hospital's "quiet room." I was in a hyperanxious mood and unfamiliar with how agitated it made me. The staff recognized it for an early manic state and asked me to step into their version of a padded cell. Except it wasn't padded.

When the door clicked shut, there was a flash of panic that had nothing to do with how I viewed myself at the moment but everything to do with a bleak memory of my first solitary confinement bid as a kid—the darkness of a cell pushed back by a bare light bulb, the black smears of dried blood and fecal matter ground into the wire mesh over the window. Though the "quiet room" here was very clean and white, I stared at the beige wire mesh covering the window like a dark rabbit hole into my past.

The maniacal rage that had simmered beneath my lungs all day sped up my heart and crawled beneath my skin. It would have been reasonable to laugh or scream or cry in abject misery. Normal to pour out my heart to some willing ear. Instead, I rammed the wall with my head. Anything to stop this confusion of fragmented thoughts crowding my mind.

In the hallway, residents were telling me to calm down, which only made me angry.

"Let me out!" I screamed. "I haven't done anything!"

No response. I beat the plexiglass window with my forehead, rattling the door in its hinges.

After the residents were shooed to their rooms, a cute nurse appeared in front of the door.

"Calm down and back away from the door," she urged.

When I complied, four burly orderlies rushed in, smothered me under a mattress, and sedated me with a needle to the hip. Then they put me in four-point restraints on the bed. I fought as much as possible given the circumstances, remembering the kids beaten in solitary, remembering the craving to feel the hot grill of a Mack truck pressed to my face. Then the needle hit me again, and it was down the rabbit hole to the words, "Calm down . . ."

The next time I was aware of anything, I was drooling, my face pressed against the cool window of a speeding cruiser. I couldn't move my upper body and finally noticed the straitjacket. It didn't worry me, though; nothing did. I closed my eyes and drifted peacefully with not a thought.

52

Helpless

Psycho sat on the dayroom floor, crying. He was a young black guy, kinda small, with pointy ears and geeky glasses. That's how come we called him Psycho. A few days earlier, before his arrest, his shotgun had misfired and blown off two toes. His bandages weren't being changed, and his foot had gotten infected.

Psycho had complained, but none of the officers seemed to care. Finally, this heavyset white deputy decided to lock him up—I guess to shut him up. "Get up and go to the holding cell!"

Psycho said he wasn't going nowhere till they got the goddamn nurse. That pissed off the officer.

"OK, that's it. Everybody go to your cells. Everybody, lock it down!" Then he marched into the control booth.

"Lockdown. Red pod, lockdown," the intercom announced. As men started trudging to their cells, I saw the nervous anxiety etched into Psycho's face. How could I walk away? What if that were me who needed assistance?

I knelt beside him. "Look, bruh, they callin' for a lockdown, which means they gonna call for 'all available.' When those guys come, they ain't coming to do no talking or extend any peace treaties. So, unless you lookin' for a fight, you might as well go to that holding cell."

Psycho kept shaking his head as if trying to resist the thought of giving up.

"Listen, if you go to lockup, maybe you'll get the medical attention you need."

Finally, he reluctantly agreed.

I pressed the intercom button to notify the deputy in the control booth to open the pod door so Psycho could comply with the order.

"Go to your cell!" the officer ordered.

"I ain't going nowhere," I responded. "Not until you get this man some medical treatment or open the door so he can go to the holding cell."

The officer cut off the intercom and pressed the all-call button. A minute later, twenty deputies piled up at the entrance.

All the other inmates had gone to their cells except me, Psycho, and one other young black man. I hadn't meant to make a stand. But I couldn't leave now. It would be cowardly.

The lieutenant told me to put my hands behind my back. I said, "This man needs medical attention. Look at his foot."

He yelled again for us to put our hands behind our backs. When the other young black man complied, several deputies seized a fistful of his hair and slammed his face against the concrete wall, then jacked his arms up high, forcing him onto his tiptoes.

I was shocked. Police were men of honor. How could they treat another human being like this? The inmate hadn't resisted. What were they going to do to me, the one who had caused the trouble? Without thinking, my fist smashed into the guard.

Pandemonium broke loose. With the force of a dozen linemen, the guards slammed me against the wall, then yanked me to the cold concrete floor.

"Get the motherfucker!" one of the deputies yelled, and a three-hundred-pound white deputy put me in a choke hold till my head was almost resting on my upper back. I couldn't breathe. An inch more and I knew my neck would snap.

"You son of a bitch, you don't ever hit an officer! We'll kill your goddamn ass in here, boy!"

Immediately, the others began punching me in the head and face. The deputy who was choking me started raking my eyeballs and sticking two fingers into my nostrils like he was trying to rip my nose apart. They kept pummeling me as the blood spilled from my mouth and nose. My vision started to dim. I realized I was about to die.

Suddenly, I was slammed against the wall with my hands still cuffed behind my back. My ankles were slapped into leg irons and my handcuffs zip-tied behind me to the ankle irons, leaving me on my stomach, unable to move. As I lay there, hogtied, on my metal bunk with no mattress and my entire weight pressing into my unprotected sternum, I began to weep.

I was nineteen years old. Awaiting trial. I hadn't even been convicted of a crime.

I thought law enforcement was there to serve and protect you, even from your own foolishness. I believed I was under the protection of their moral authority. I held these men to a higher standard. But I realized now they could do anything to me and get away with it. The guards who didn't participate just stood by and watched.

They stripped me of my clothes that day, but they also stripped me of my illusions. Ain't nobody gonna protect you from those sworn to serve.

And that "nobody" includes me. If I'm watching somebody getting staples in their head, teeth knocked out, I don't say nothing, 'cause if I do, I might be next. I just climb in my bed, pull the covers over my head.

Helpless.

53

Just Like a Frog

You know the craziest thing about being eighteen and in jail?

Me neither.

Our cellblock was full of crazy people made crazier by twenty-three hours a day in solitary. We were all at the county jail, awaiting sentencing. Four others were facing death sentences. Mitchell, a pasty-looking man, believed there were listening devices in the air ducts and refused to talk above a whisper. During his hour of rec, he skittered around, muttering to the others. Small Paul, another juvenile, was wild and angry, despite handfuls of meds. He shaped his pain into a weapon, banging on the door or commode and screaming. D-Rod passed his time making animal noises or wrestling with his mattress. And Johnnyboy sang and danced to imaginary music day and night. I don't think he ever slept.

Come to think of it, I *do* know the craziest thing: this wasn't even the psych ward.

After a year in solitary, it's a miracle I wasn't crowin' too. Self-hatred and depression gnawed at me. I grieved for the victims. I grieved for my short, wasted life. The familiar cracks in the wall seemed like a meaningless road map with only one exit.

One night, I decided to take that exit. I stripped the sheet from my bunk and tore it in half lengthwise. One end I tied to the bar over the window, the other around my neck in a slipknot. Because the window was so high, I stood on my rolled-up mattress, took a deep breath, then kicked the mattress to the floor. My bare feet flailed against the wall as I choked.

Shit fabric, probably had a thread count of three. It ripped in half. I lay on the floor, gasping.

The next day during rec, I left my cell, ignoring D-Rod's rooster impression, and climbed the stairs with my towel, as if heading for the shower. When I got to the top tier, I stood by the rail. Twenty-five feet to concrete.

I dove headfirst.

I guess it was instinct. My arms and legs shot forward and turned that headlong dive into a half-assed roll. It was incredibly painful. Two broken arms. Worse, though, was the utter shame of another failure in a life full of them. There would be no easy escape from that.

My high-flying act didn't go unpunished. It caused the staff a lot of paperwork, not to mention a trip to the hospital. When I returned, I was stripped naked and shackled to a bunk with the AC on high. A few hours later, a paper gown slid beneath the door. For showers, they handcuffed me while a guard watched. If I refused to shower, they threatened to use a fire hose. I knew it wasn't an idle threat; I'd already seen it done to a Mexican kid. During my one hour of rec, I was taken to a table in the dayroom and shackled there.

What I didn't expect was Mitchell, Small Paul, D-Rod, Johnnyboy— they all came to check on me. Small Paul even calmed down enough to say, "Man, you're crazy! I didn't think you'd do it. Then, next thing I know, you're flying through the air! You looked just like a frog." He paused. "Except, I got to say, they land better."

I had to laugh. It was odd to feel camaraderie in this refuse bin where we'd all been discarded like so much trash. But that's what it was. We'd been cast off, but we weren't alone.

54

The Source

When I was in the county jail awaiting trial, I would wait till after lockup to read any mail I received. I wouldn't even look to see who wrote me. I'd just toss it under my bunk. I'd discovered that, more often than not, if I read their letters right before going to sleep, I would dream about the people who wrote. I would dream about being free.

It had been many months since coming to jail, and I had come to grips with the fact that my so-called friends had moved on. Only my family and one girl were holding me down. It hurt like hell, but I was dealing with it. Well, one night, I found that an old high school friend had wrote! I hadn't seen or heard from him in years. We were hip-hop junkies together back in the day, and the *Source* magazine was our crack.

"I wasn't sure if they would let me send you the whole mag," he said in the letter, "so I just shot you a few pages."

More than half of the book had been ripped out and sent. It was the most kind and thoughtful thing anyone had done for me in a long time. I had no choice but to thank God that I had a single cell as I sat there crying while I finished his letter.

This was a friend I didn't deserve. When we were sixteen, he became a father, and upon hearing the news, he stepped right up to the plate. He was the most responsible guy I knew. I also knew his baby's mother, and since she seemed cool and he was trying to do the family thing, I fell back. Let him do his thing.

Looking back now, I see that I was wrong. He probably needed a friend more than ever. Lord knows, he's been one to me. To this day, he remains the only male who has ever written to me. I also still have one page of that *Source* magazine. He is exactly what he said he was in that letter: my brother for life. Wherever you are, thank you, my friend.

55

I Heard You

I never got an opportunity to thank him. It's taken me a while to mature and to be able to appreciate the depth of his kindness. I was twenty-one; it was my first time in prison. I wanted to show everyone I was a badass, and I was determined to be my worst.

As a teenager, I'd begun experimenting with drugs, and the effects of PCP ravaged my brain, turning me into a person even I couldn't recognize. By the time I met this officer, those effects were beginning to wane, and I was confronted with the horror that had become my life.

My mother always had such high hopes for me, and I'd squandered everything. Sitting in a maximum-security prison, it dawned on me that I had hit rock bottom. The fact that she still adored me somehow seemed to make things worse. Guilt made it difficult to breathe. I became overwhelmed with shame, and I guess I was having a panic attack.

He asked me what was the matter. Vulnerable, desperate, and genuinely afraid, I blurted out everything. The more hysterical I became, the more calm and reassuring were his words. He told me not to worry, that there were programs available.

It may not seem like much; he probably doesn't even remember it. But it was a pivotal moment in my life. That's when my thinking changed. I changed what was in my heart and began to do things differently. By then, I'd already been in a couple fights and was nearly killed in a riot ignited by gang violence. After that, guys no longer came at me with drugs and weapons—they asked me for help with their schoolwork so that they could pass their GED tests, and my mom's smile was less troubled during our visits. It was still a bad place, and I was filled with regrets, but I was doing positive things and moving in the right direction. So it was a pretty big deal to me.

I wish I could tell him: those times when you called me, and I kept walking; I heard you. I knew you wanted me to tuck my shirttail in; I knew it was against the rules to have it out. I had no issue with you. I was just mad at myself and mad at the world. You never took it personally, or you seemed not to. Even when I cussed you and forced you to write me up, you took it all in stride. Although your face got awfully red, you were always a professional.

One time, I went outside in the pouring rain, and he came out about thirty minutes later holding an umbrella. I knew he didn't want to be out there. I'm sure he'd gotten a call from the guard in the gun tower asking, "Why is this fool outside in the rain?"

He asked me what I was doing. I said I'd just purchased some Gore-Tex boots and was testing them to see if they were indeed waterproof.

The expression on his face was the universal look of one who realizes they're dealing with a special case. Trust me, I knew I had issues. But he left me to my experiment. (By the way, the boots worked as advertised.) Maybe it's hard to understand, but I was just so happy and proud to own something that wasn't state-issued.

I never forgot his kindness. On the night of my panic attack, things could've gotten progressively worse for me. And during that riot, that knife was only inches away from my torso. Not a shank, a kitchen knife; I still remember the sun gleaming off the long blade. But with his help, I was able to go the other way. I was a black kid from the inner city. He was a white country boy from the mountains. But we were just people. I needed him, and he was there.

56

Mercy on My Soul

It took the jury only four hours to determine my fate.

My mother sat right behind me, holding tight to my little sister's hand. They were the only people in the world who cared enough about me to show up.

The victim's family sat behind the prosecutor. A grandmother and mother. Both had lost a man they called son. Behind the grandmother's large-framed glasses, her eyes seemed quiet and kind. I thought her face showed mercy.

The mother's face did not. Her eyes were daggers of hatred. I couldn't bear to meet them, my heart was so heavy with guilt.

So I focused on the judge. He fanned out the sides of his robe like some superhero's cape. "The jury, having found the defendant guilty of murder in the first degree, sentence him to death. . . ."

My mother screamed. My little sister started wailing. He kept talking, but his words became background chatter. I seemed to be watching from outside myself, like my soul was hovering above me, trying to escape.

The judge asked each juror to stand one by one and affirm their verdict. I watched in a daze as the figures seesawed up and down. Suddenly, there was a pause.

A black woman remained seated after her name was called. She choked back heavy sobs.

My heart raised up a little. Was there hope?

The juror to her right tenderly stroked the woman's back. Gripping her chair, the woman looked at me, and a sob erupted that wracked her whole body. She struggled to her feet, took a breath, and uttered a weak "Yes." Then she collapsed into her seat, weeping.

It moved me. I almost wanted to thank her, to console her myself. It touched my heart that even though this woman had sentenced me to death, she recognized my humanity and it caused her so much pain.

The judge peered down at me, the look on his face total condemnation. He brought down the gavel like a weapon. "MAY GOD HAVE MERCY ON YOUR SOUL!"

57

Butterflies

Pale green, eyespots on its hind wings
A long tail—the luna moth only flies
At night. On cloudless nights
When moonlight strikes, it seems to glow
(like an eerie spirit) near black walnut
Trees to lay its eggs on the underbelly
Of leaves. As a larva it crawls around
Feeding greedily, intuiting its inevitable
Famine. By nature, it wraps itself in
Silk threads that become its prison.
A luna moth—the imago—emerges
From its cocoon on a day two weeks
From its pupation. Without a mouth.
It will not eat. It will live for one
Week, then die: it spends longer getting
Born than being alive, than begetting
More pale-green light that flies.
I learned of this during my murder
Trial, realizing butterfly metaphors
Can describe the degenerative rapacity
Of street pharmacists—whose deaths
Can be the mother of their beauty.

Though I was twenty-five, somehow I was
Also both old and wombed.
During my trial's sentencing phase,
The prosecutor cross-examined my ex
Of our life together at twenty, the image
Of broke, at the edge of my ambition.
Everybody questioned her testimony:
We were so tired of only eating
ramen noodles. We craved anything
from Wendy's but we had only, like,
four dollars. We could share a value meal.
He said he wasn't hungry,
So I ate all of it. But then, at home,
He ate a ramen. It was the sweetest
Thing anyone had ever done for me. I groaned,
Because I had completely forgotten
Who I used to be and could be once
Again. Once sentenced to death
I sighed: no longer having to live
The hustler's life of living to have
Gave me butterflies.

58

After the Storm

After a long day of testimony at my capital murder trial, I looked out the window to see my mom hugging the mother of the victim. For me, it was like a rainbow after the storm. She said she just wanted to apologize to them because she could feel their hurt and pain. She wanted them to know that we, myself included, were so sorry for their loss.

And she wanted mercy and forgiveness for her own child. She said it was easy because they were so forgiving.

The next day, when the jury went to deliberate my sentence, the bailiffs put me in a holding cell to wait. I hadn't been there ten minutes when the bailiffs came back saying I needed to return to court.

I said, "There's no way the jury came back this quick."

They said, "No. Your mother needs you."

We walked back to court. They didn't even bother to handcuff me, I'd been there so long, almost four years waiting for my trial. We'd developed a level of trust. We walked into the courtroom. My mom was with my attorney's assistants. She was wailing inconsolably.

I said, "Aw, Mom . . ." The bailiffs and deputies let me sit with her. "It's OK, it's OK," I told her, kissing the hands that have worked so hard all her life. She'd done all she could her whole life, and now all she could do was cry. I comforted and kissed her until she calmed down a little. Letting me sit with her was a real kindness; I still say prayers for those men and their families.

For me, the death verdict was anticlimactic, but it almost killed my mother. She went into shock. She had never touched a drop of alcohol in her life, but after the sentencing, she had to be hospitalized for alcohol poisoning. She hovered for weeks on the brink between life and death. And then . . . she got back up, just like she'd been doing her whole life.

On one of our rare visits, I noticed her hands shaking. The plexiglass partition kept me from reaching out to hold them. Cautiously, I asked her why she was shaking.

"Baby, when I think about your situation, I have to pretend you're just in prison doing time," she said. "When I think about the actual circumstances, I can't function. Even before I was touched by it, I thought the death penalty was barbaric and wrong. God-fearing people don't do stuff like that. It's hypocritical to say we are Christians who believe in a God of forgiveness and then turn around and kill people. It don't make sense. I promise I'll try to do better, but it just scares me to death."

Then she brightened. "But I have good news."

"What?" I asked, smiling.

"I'm cancer-free," she said excitedly.

"Huh?" I was dumbfounded. I thought I'd misheard. "You had cancer?! Why didn't you tell me?"

"I didn't want to worry you," she answered with a mischievous grin, then added, "God is so good."

Yet another rainbow. But this one after a storm I wasn't even around to feel. If a rainbow can be bittersweet, this was it.

VI

Worst of the Worst

(ENTERING DEATH ROW AND SOLITARY)

What You Got?

Still handcuffed, I was led to a cell-sized holding room. Two guys were already inside. One was wearing his prison browns, but the guy across from me wore street clothes like myself.

"What you got, dog?" he asked.

Still numb, I replied, "Death."

"Damn," he said. "You're so young."

I just nodded. An officer passed him what looked like two small folded paper bags and a string. One white, one brown. The guy started taking off his street clothes.

While he was undressing, the man in browns went over to the toilet, pulled down his pants, and sat. It shocked me out of my stupor. This really was prison. Everything I'd ever heard about the place flooded my mind. I glanced toward the other guy and could see now what the paper packets had held: two brown paper flip-flops and a white paper gown.

I pulled off my tie.

An officer came for the older man in browns. As they were leaving, Browns said, "Look, I don't know where they're sending you, but here." He gave me two dollars, half a striker, four matches, and four cigarettes. "Split the matches; they'll last longer."

Then he turned as they walked out the door. "Hang in there; it's not over yet."

Worst of the Worst

I'd just spent twenty-two months in a county jail. Stabbing, beating, and stealing was as common as the sunrise. So I could only imagine how magnified that would be on death row. I mean, the people in jail were there on trespassing, larceny, misdemeanor charges. The men on death row, they'd all been condemned for taking at least one life. They were the "worst of the worst," right? I knew it would be a vicious place to live.

I arrived near midnight.

The very next moment, a prisoner approached me. He introduced himself and asked if I smoked. When I said yes, he gave me tobacco and coffee and then explained that in order to listen to the TV, I had to have a radio.

OK, I was new here. He didn't owe me anything. So what was his *real* motive? Plus, I was white, and he was black. What did he really want?

I found out. What he really wanted was to give me a radio and the money to purchase headphones for it. It was simply a genuine act of kindness.

It shook up my whole perception of other people. And of myself. In the free world, I rarely witnessed acts of kindness; I could probably count all of them on maybe two hands. I discovered that on death row, kindness and compassion are everyday occurrences. No one really gives it a thought; it's just second nature.

When you see somebody do something nice for someone, you know deep down inside that you're the same type of person. You want to do something nice for somebody. But I might not have done it before because of my fears of how other people could perceive that.

Well, preconceived notions can be shattered.

61

Nursing Home

The floor was gray. Not gloomy. Not cheerful. Just quiet. The walls were white. Almost as if they had been bleached. Not what I expected in a unit built to house death. This wasn't how I'd envisioned the ugliness of death. Where were the blood-streaked walls with bloody handprints? The smudges from cigarettes, or roaches, or flies? I immediately distrusted it, as if someone had spent hours scrubbing to rid it of the stench of death. I wondered briefly if someone had just frantically mopped up the blood and the vomit in preparation for my arrival.

The hallway just looked medicinal. It was strangely businesslike—a hospital or doctor's office.

Suddenly, a black woman appeared from an office, her hair fashioned in a trendy style. She wore a sergeant's stripes on her shoulder. I had expected a bull of a cop who only spoke the language of aggression to meet me at the gates of death. I was surprised to see this harmless middle-aged woman with all the fussiness of a mother hen. She assigned me a cell location and escorted me to where I was housed.

I scanned the faces as I entered the unit for the condemned, the "worst of the worst," and was shocked at what I found. An old black man in a wheelchair with an aluminum prosthetic leg staring at the TV with a glassy look in his eyes. A white man, who looked to be about sixty but who clearly had the mind of a child, playing checkers with a black man just like him. Two children in the bodies of old men, playing a game while waiting to die.

I put my belongings in my cell. Maybe a nursing home was a kind of death row, but it sure wasn't the one I was expecting.

62

Combat Readiness

I was buck naked in the middle of a ten-by-twenty-foot cell with nothing but a bare mattress, a pair of paper flip-flops, and a toilet.

Three hours earlier, I'd been standing in court, awaiting sentencing. The judge announced I would receive a life sentence. Whew!

And also, he informed me, a death sentence. Life for one crime and death for the other. I couldn't take it in. How was that supposed to work? Didn't one sort of cancel out the other? I was so shook up, they gave me a massive dose of anti-anxiety drugs just to calm me down. Then, inside prison, they gave me more.

So there I was, completely naked, standing in an empty room with nothing but a bare mattress, a pair of paper flip-flops, and a toilet. I was so pumped full of meds, I thought that room was death row. I thought that's where I had to stay until they came to execute me.

I grabbed the paper flip-flops. How was I gonna kill myself with those? I looked around the room in desperation and got an idea: the toilet! If I could make it across the room, I could do a handstand over the toilet bowl, throw out my arms, and *bam!* I'd either snap my neck and die, or I'd conk out and drown in the water.

But then I started to worry—what if I survived with a broken neck? Or just knocked myself out? Not to mention, the walls suddenly seemed to be moving. Then the floor, too. I wasn't sure I could even get across the room in this state.

I folded the bare mattress like a trifold wallet and settled onto it. At some point, I must have dozed off.

Suddenly, I woke with a start. Something was very wrong. My skin was crawling. I leaped up. Something was all over me, all over my arms and legs.

Roaches! The walls and floors weren't moving; they were covered in thousands of roaches.

There was nowhere to take cover. I grabbed the paper flip-flops and went into combat readiness mode. By sunrise, I'd killed enough to make a pile that stretched four feet long and was two inches deep. Dead roaches upon dead roaches . . .

I guess I went a little crazy then. I started screaming. But already I knew, help was not on the way.

63

The Hole

The Hole is where I learned what it really means to give up.

I'd been sent to solitary confinement while they investigated some bogus charge. Solitary confinement—aka the Hole.

The first thing that hits you is the noise—screaming men mule-kicking steel doors. *Bam! Bam! Bam!* Someone yelling, "Gimme my damn blanket! Gimme my damn blanket!" *Bam! Bam!*

The next thing that assaults you is the stench. Human waste and unwashed bodies. I gagged.

My cell contained an empty mattress and a slit window covered by a steel grate. As the guard removed my handcuffs through a slot in the door, he shouted that the previous occupant had died two days earlier.

Just then a man started yelling at the screamer, "Shut up! You stupid son of a bitch! Shut up!"

Sometimes the screaming went on for hours before the guy went hoarse or was beaten nearly to death by the guards. Sometimes the screaming sounded more like an animal in pain than a human. Howling, rabid, slobbering. What else is left when you're naked and chained to a cold metal bunk smeared in your own filth?

There were prisoners who swallowed batteries or squirreled away pieces of concrete and hardened paint chips to mutilate their bodies. Some drove pens or pencils into their genitals. Basically, anything to leave the Hole or to be touched by a human being.

When one of those prisoners had to be removed, the extraction team would arrive decked out in riot gear, with shock shields and batons and canisters of mace the size of fire extinguishers.

The smell of mace and feces came in cycles. Maybe a hallucination brought out the screaming, or one prisoner antagonized another from their cell. Morning, noon, and night: "Shut up!" *Bam! Bam! Bam!*

They were broken men. Many had lost all connection to the world. Some had been in the Hole for so many years, it was the only home they remembered. Others were so doped up on meds, they couldn't recognize what was going on.

Where there's no hope, there's no sanity. Or maybe it's the other way around. It doesn't matter. The Hole is a place without either one.

64

Peanut

When I finally arrived in prison, I was in very bad shape emotionally, mentally, and physically. I was an addict, angry, frustrated, and in denial. I was a complete mess. While sitting in my cell, thinking about the innocent life I took and the pain I had caused many, including God, I quickly fell into a very dark and deep well of depression from which I could see no way out.

My prison cell had the usual bars, but the front of the cell was also covered with a heavy steel, diamond-patterned screen. With no window or paint, it felt like I was locked in a dungeon.

One day, this little mouse came wandering into my cell, looking for an easy snack. This was my happiest moment ever! I broke off a piece of cracker and put it on the floor. He quickly grabbed it and was off in a furry flash.

Minutes later, he was back. After several times of having my new friend scamper off with chunks of food, leaving me with no company, I decided to give him smaller pieces in the hope he would stay and eat instead of leaving to store the morsel.

It worked! By the next day, he was even eating small pieces of food from my fingers. Soon after, he started climbing onto the palm of my hand and happily eating his treats there. He'd sit on his hind legs, proudly holding his food with his tiny front claws, and stare at me, while I sat on my bed and had a serious conversation with him.

Clearly, I was the talker. He seemed content to just nibble and listen to my nonstop chatter. Only when I stopped talking did his nibbling and whiskers come to a complete halt.

My favorite thing to do was rub peanuts on the tips of my fingers. He would lightly grab a fingertip with his teeth and tug and pull with all his might in hopes of taking this giant morsel to his secret hiding place. When he finally realized my finger wasn't going anywhere, he'd sit on his hind legs and firmly hold each finger with his tiny claws as he licked the delicious salt and oil from its tip.

For almost a month, he was my little buddy. He distracted me just long enough to get me through the darkest, loneliest, most unstable time in my life. That tiny creature was an unexpected angel. His presence reminded me that we are all children of God. We all have value and purpose, however small we may feel.

65

Motel 6

I was escorted down a long, dank, dark hallway and placed inside a holding cell. From behind the closed main door, I could hear a muffled "Blue!"

Guys were yelling from behind their cell doors, "Blue! Blue!" They knew I was there. All I could do was holler back in acknowledgment. I couldn't make out what was said, but I recognized their voices and was immediately arrested by regret. I'd known these other men from death row were in isolation but had forgotten about them. I was surprised how quickly they could be erased from my thoughts. It made me think of all the people who had forgotten me over the years. I forgave them on the spot and vowed to myself not to forget again.

A guard recognized me and asked if it was my first time on the isolation unit. I told her it was.

"What did you do?" she asked.

"I have no idea," I answered truthfully. I was still a bit stunned.

"Well, sorry, but this down here is the Motel 6. It's filthy."

Two other officers arrived. The first said enthusiastically, "We got a cell for you," as if he took great pride in fast service.

His partner added, "But it's pretty fucked up. Will you take it?"

For a moment, I was taken aback. Did I have a choice?

"Is there another available?" I asked.

There wasn't. The guard kicked a mound of trash out of the cell and gave me some all-purpose cleaner and a rag. I took off my jumpsuit to keep it clean, tore the rag in half, and went to work. By the time I had finished, the rags were black, but the cell was definitely cleaner.

High up, a narrow window covered in painted metal promised a view of the sky, but the holes in the metal mesh were too small, and some sort of opaque coating covered the glass. Someone had gone to great effort to ensure no occupant ever saw grass or sky.

I overheard a man in another cell say he'd gotten there the day before and didn't yet have his personal property. Another man said he'd been there a week and still didn't have his. With that information, I put my jumpsuit back on and went to sleep on the bare mattress.

The next day, I received written notification that I was being held on a forty-five-day investigation and would not be getting my property. I didn't really see how my stamps, shampoo, toothpaste, or deodorant could be pertinent to some investigation, but I just requested my ID card so I could purchase those necessities.

My request was denied.

After a week without showering or brushing my teeth, I gave up and just decided my body odor had a bit of personality.

I also decided not to participate in our one hour of "rec," which consisted of being handcuffed, strip-searched, and then locked inside a massive black metal cage in the dayroom area. All you could do in the cage was pace or do push-ups, and I could do those in my cell without the humiliation of public nudity.

But I ended up locked in a cage for outside "rec." A kid a couple cages down was still in full restraints, hands and feet shackled, even though he was locked inside a steel cage. The kid seemed like one of the nicest guys, but he said he even had to wear restraints when he showered. He'd figured out the most effective way of getting clean was to soap himself in his cell so when he got to the shower, all he had to do was rinse.

To an outside observer, I imagined all of us in this row of cages looked just like dogs kenneled in some animal shelter.

Back inside, I found the man in the cell next to mine was also from death row. He offered to buy me a honey bun and a radio. "I know this is your first time down here. Man, I'm used to this shit."

I thanked him and declined. I said all I needed was an international stamp to write my baby; it was my only concern. I needed my family to know where I was.

He said he didn't have a stamp.

Then I heard another voice calling me. It was the kid in full restraints. "Blue! If you ain't got your stuff by the time we go to canteen, I'll get you an international stamp. Not to worry."

I was moved by their kindness. Whatever issues these guys had, and they might be legion, they wore them well.

66

All These Guys

Yes, there are some correctional officers who will handcuff a guy and then shove him down the stairs. Or cuff a guy in an area where there aren't any cameras and beat him half to death. Those officers mistreat men just because they can, just because they have the "authority." There's some officers should be on this side of the bars, for sure.

But there's other men who earn our respect because they treat everyone with respect. This one guard, he was never promoted to the rank of sergeant or lieutenant, probably because he didn't want it. But he had the power and respect of those ranks. He didn't let a negative experience with one prisoner affect his attitude toward the rest. He had positive relationships with guys. And by "positive," I don't mean he turned men into snitches and collaborators in exchange for reduced sentences. These were true positive relationships. Those who carried themselves respectfully, he treated or dealt with likewise.

I was in a hearing board meeting where they were deciding whether I would get off lockup, solitary confinement. His coworkers didn't want to let me off lockup because they said I was a Blood gangbanger.

But this officer interceded on my behalf, saying, "He ain't no gang member—he's a Muslim. I know all of these guys, and he ain't no Blood."

They had me step out while they spoke with him. After a minute, I was called back in and was given the glad tidings that I was getting off of lockup!

I wish there were more officers like him, old-school officers, not afraid to speak up, even for the men who are on the other side of the line. Truth is truth and right is right, no matter who it's coming from.

67

Word Is Bond

I was pacing my cell when there was a sharp tap on the door.

"You're going to see the Captain." In moments, my trapdoor opened, and I heard the click of handcuffs jangling outside my door.

Resigned, I began taking off my clothes. Standard procedure before exiting the cell: strip to my boxers, hand my clothes to the guard through the trapdoor, and leave my hands there to be cuffed. The guard would then escort me to a holding cell where I would be uncuffed, remove my boxers, raise my arms to expose my armpits, open my mouth, turn, squat, cough, and lift the soles of my feet before my clothes were returned to me.

Surprisingly, I was told to leave my clothes on. Once I was handcuffed through the trapdoor, my cell door was opened, and three guards marched me to an office where two captains and the Deputy Warden waited.

"Take those cuffs off him, and you all step outside," the Warden said to the guards.

I was without restraints in the presence of other human beings for the first time in seven and a half years. I felt a surge of fear mixed with awkward viciousness, as if I were supposed to attack them. Like a dog who had been chained to a tree for years, I felt a dangerous sense of freedom, with no notion how to use it.

The Warden smiled at me. Didn't he realize that I was supposed to be in restraints? Did he think that after seven and a half years in a cage, and all that I had seen and done, he could sit me down and we could be civil?

"I have a recommendation to let you off lockup," he said.

I almost fell to the floor. Of all the possible scenarios running through my mind, this one blindsided me.

"Tell me, please, why should I do that?" he continued.

I was speechless. I had given up years ago on ever being let out of solitary. Although every six months I came up for review, I was always denied for the same reason: my prior history of violence. No matter what I did, my history would forever be the same. Yet here I was in a face-to-face meeting without restraints. It was a test. If I couldn't be civil in this office, then I didn't deserve to be let off lockup.

I sucked in my breath and removed my inner mask. "Because I've done my time."

"That's fair enough. You've been on lockup for about eight years?"

"Seven and a half."

"How can you convince me that if I let you off lockup, you won't do something like this again?"

Without missing a beat, I said, "I don't think there's anything I can say to convince you. All I can do is ask you to look at my conduct the past seven years and let that speak on my behalf."

Silence. Then he started again. "Well, here's my other concern. We've got some executions coming up. Nothing personal, just business. You have a history as some kind of leader. You organized a hunger strike a few years ago, and, well, I don't want you to get out there and put any ideas in these guys' minds. I believe you are the type of man that stands by his word, what they call a Convict. And if you give a man your word, you'll keep it. Can you give me your word that if I let you off lockup, you won't try and rile these guys up? Because I don't need that to deal with. We've got death row the way we want it, and I intend for it to stay that way."

I was shocked. I couldn't believe he was asking me to somehow be complicit in ensuring that those waiting to die were not agitated. I had no intention of organizing any large-scale movement, but I certainly wouldn't be his co-conspirator in death.

He continued, "We just opened a brand-new unit for you guys with your own rec yard—basketball, volleyball, weight lifting. The building is clean, lots of space. You get a movie once a week. And on the pods, guys play dominoes and chess and checkers. I just don't need you putting any thoughts in these guys' heads. Can you give me your word?"

Still shocked, I nodded. It seemed less binding that way. He had the gall to tell me that this was business, nothing personal, and that he had death row like he wanted it. Games and diversions to distract the condemned from focusing on ideas "in their heads," such as the fact that they were waiting to be executed.

On top of that, he had the nerve to call me into some closed-door meeting as if I were the only man on the inside who knew what was really going on. And then ensnare me by forcing me to compromise my integrity or remain on lockup.

"Is that your word?" he asked again.

"Yeah, that's my word," I finally said. I would decide later on how honest I was. But today, I was getting off lockup.

VII

You Are Not Here to Be Rehabilitated

(LIFE ON DEATH ROW)

68

The Raw

My first six months on house arrest, I had to go to night school. This girl asked me did I have any aspirations. Nobody ever asked me that before. I didn't have nothing to say. One of my parole conditions was I had to work, and one morning I didn't want to cut grass, so I didn't go. I got a write-up. This man on the parole board said, "You serving a life sentence and you don't even know it."

He was right. Two months later, I was back inside. But I didn't understand what he meant. I mean, it's a great line: "You serving a life sentence and you don't even know it." But I'm like: ELABORATE!

All I hear is you disrespecting me. Forget prophesizing my future. Tell me what you mean. Break it down.

I mean, you can't be *re*-habilitated if you ain't never been habilitated in the first place.

'Cause I had no idea what change was. You know, old folks always saying, "You better change your ways," and I'm like, "Yeah. Imma change. I ain't drinking no more Thunderbird—that bird always get me in trouble. From now on, I'm only drinking *beer!*"

Folks try and scare you, like how you're gonna get gang-raped in prison or someone's gonna cut you. But I was raised up hard. I can take care of myself. Nobody tells you about the utter monotony, the abject misery, the daily slog. What it's like to wash your clothes in the same pot you piss in, to have ten minutes to eat, constant interrupted sleep. They don't say how trapped you'll feel, day after day, year after year, staring at concrete walls with no one coming to visit.

Nobody tells you how you're gonna break your mama's heart. Wreck your kids' lives. My father was in prison my whole life. I wonder, did he ever want to tell me how it hurt his heart being gone? I haven't seen my own son in twelve years. I write, send cards, but I knew the moment the police handcuffed me it was over. He'd grow up alone, and I'd never get to be the father I could have been.

They don't tell you how much you're gonna miss your family. I haven't hugged my mom in twenty years. But she come to visit, and I get all dressed up, brush my teeth, comb my hair, like it's some big reunion. Why? That ain't how I look. That ain't how I feel. This is a miserable, miserable existence. You need to hear the raw. It hurts being here. I am distressed. I ain't OK. It's torture to be dead and alive to know it.

Firstborn

I never heard your first cry. I never smelled your first poop, never had the chance to clean you up. I never had the blessing to cradle your newborn, good-smelling baby flesh in the palms of my hands.

I've had to learn you from hundreds of miles on one hand and from inches through wire-reinforced glass on the other.

I've watched you grow and mature from your drawings to your young adult handwriting.

I've followed your life through twenty years of photos. We've been told that a picture can say a thousand words. That's a damn lie! A smell, a touch can speak a thousand words, not a flat, lifeless photo of my beloved. I want to hold you, feel your weight, and trace the contours of your face. I want to smell your skin and hair, the aroma of your breath as you laugh.

I can't enjoy none of this, and neither can you, from a picture, letter, or visitation through a wall of plexiglass and wire.

We need some contact, physical contact, to truly connect.

Valentine's Day

Me and Kit grew up together. Her papaw and mine were best friends. They worked at the sawmill together. Our moms were best friends, too. We knew each other since birth, basically. We sucked each other's mama's tits.

Me and Kit used to hang out in the woods, swamps, marshes. One time, we were fishing in a marsh and spotted something wriggling just beneath the surface. It was a baby alligator, about eight inches long. I'd tried to catch them before but never could. So I wanted to try again. I wasn't scared. Small as that hatchling was, it couldn't hardly hurt me. I speared my hand in a couple times until I caught it. It just froze. It didn't resist or try to bite me. It had no experience with humans. I wanted to keep it as a pet.

At least until Monday. We decided to take it to school. We had caught other things and brung 'em to school. Chipmunks, mostly. But we were actually thinking to catch a bear or bobcat. We had a small box trap, probably only big enough to catch a rabbit. We didn't know any better. Papaw had tried to scare us by telling us to stay out of the woods because there were bobcats and bears in there. We of course immediately decided to catch one. All we caught was chipmunks.

Monday morning, we walked to school as usual. We were a pair, I tell you. Both so skinny. We generally wore cowboy boots and hat, she in a dress, me in jeans and T-shirt. We even wore cap-gun six-shooters. Anyway, I put on a jacket and hid the gator under it, sort of cradling it till we got to school. I went to my desk in back, and the other kids knew I had something, but not what. They crowded round, giggling, looking back and forth between me and the teacher up front. She could tell something was up. That's when I set him down.

He just stood there a second, looking around. Once the other kids realized what it was, some shrieked and climbed up on their chairs. The gator took off, scrambling around the room till it reached a wall. I was worried somebody might stomp on him, so I stayed nearby.

The teacher screamed, then ran out of the room hollerin'. A male teacher down the hall came out, and she grabbed him. But when he seen that gator, he screamed just as loud and ran for help. Somebody said he was calling the police and Animal Control. That's when I scooped up my gator and took off. Climbed right out the window, over to the marshes, and set him free.

When we got to be thirteen, the doctor discovered cysts on Kit's fallopian tubes. Ended up having to have a hysterectomy. A couple years later, she was like, "Look, we both know you want kids, and I can't have any. You're gonna have to find someone else."

I knew she was right. I did want to be a father; it's part of who I am. So although we loved each other to death, we weren't meant to marry. We stayed best friends.

I got married and started a family. She stayed single, happy to be my best friend.

She didn't want anybody else. I was the only person she ever slept with, and we only stopped when I committed to someone else—we had morals. But even after I married, I always had this nagging feeling in the back of my heart that I was cheating on Kit.

The year after I got convicted and sentenced to death, she committed suicide on Valentine's Day—our day. She wrote a note. Even before I read what it said, I knew. She was such a beautiful, simple woman. She ain't want much. Hell, ever since we were kids, she always just wanted to be a waitress like her mom. And she wanted me. Simple as that.

In the letter, she said she knew I was innocent. And she could not stand the thought of me being here. We'd been separated before, but I was always within reach. She could hug me, touch me. Now she couldn't. She told me she'd meet me at the Pearly Gates; she wanted to get there first and wait on me.

There have been times where I was THIS CLOSE to joining her. But each time I was on the edge, something would happen, some sort of sign to discourage me from going through with it. I'd feel this coolness move across my knees and over my shoulders, exactly the same way Kit used to ease onto my lap and lay her arm across my shoulders. I believe that's her way of letting me know she's still here with me—that everything's going to be OK.

71

Time Lost

When is a situation lost to you? How do you know?

At eighteen, seeing all these kids going to the prom—I missed all that. I felt like at eighteen you're too old for kid things, you got to take responsibility for your life. At eighteen I knew what it was like to be homeless. I knew what it was like to pay bills. I knew what life was. At eighteen you couldn't tell me nothing. Growing up with nobody caring about you, I made my own way. I was tough. But truthfully, I was just scared. I had been my whole life. Fearlessness was just a front to surviving.

"Boy, trouble is easy to get into but hard to get out of" is something I heard many times. Yet it wasn't until I was twenty-one and headed to prison that it truly registered. Losing your freedom is a shocking experience in itself, especially in those first moments. You're locked in a cell, wishing you were anyplace but there. Thoughts of regret fill your head until you're dizzy with anguish.

The mental and emotional turmoil that followed was stifling. At the time, I had a son whom I adored. The day my son was born, it was a Saturday, just moments before the "Soul Train Line" started. I doted on him as a toddler, laying him on my chest until he fell asleep. I remember spoiling him as a little boy so he could enjoy life like I never could. Never would he have to wait for the monthly food stamp check to have decent food to eat. Not my son. He would have better.

Also, contrary to my abusive actions, I was still very much in love with his mother, my beautiful wife. Being separated from them was difficult to accept. Talk about miserable. That was one of the worst feelings I'd ever had in my life.

I had always held on to the hope of being a better father, more present in my children's lives. A better man to some woman. I would put an end to my immoral and criminal ways, and everything would finally be good. That was the plan, but it fell through.

When the police handcuffed me, I knew I had just blown my last chance to be a free man—at least for a long time. My son would grow up without me, just as I had without my own father. Misery descended and has ridden me like a beast of burden for nearly two decades now. I felt as if I had died, only my body didn't know it. Worse, my mind didn't either. My whole life flashed before my eyes. So many "never agains." So much left undone.

My son, whom I love immensely, has made it clear he has no desire to communicate with me. He is angry due to both my absence from his life all these years and my emotional and physical transgressions against his mother. Over the course of the past years, I have apologized with the utmost sincerity numerous times. Yet while his mother has forgiven me, my son refuses to do so.

All he knows is that I have been gone more than five times as long as the time we spent together, and it angers him. Me, I'm deeply saddened. I had such noble intentions for my son. I would be the good father I never had. But I failed my son, and worse, there is absolutely nothing I can do about it. I could apologize a million times and he could rebuke me a million more, but nothing would change. Time lost is gone forever.

I had hoped that as my son grew into adulthood, he would understand the situation and forgive me, and perhaps someday he will.

Just not today.

72

Hugs

All my memories of my father are of him in one prison or another. I've never had the chance to see him in the free world, because he got locked up when I was only a month old.

No matter what prison he was in, though, my grandparents and I would go visit once a month. Sometimes we'd have to travel three hours each way just for a two-hour visit. But it was well worth it. We got to take pictures together, eat snacks, talk about how I was doing in school, talk about his life behind those walls, and best of all, we got to hug each other before we left.

Those two hours together were priceless. I was always kind of sad when we left, because I wanted to stay with him. He was my dad. But I was also happy, because every time we were together, we built on our relationship. And I got to hug him—sometimes I'd hug him two or three times each visit. It was just something about that hug I can't explain.

Dad would tell me to stay out of trouble and especially "Don't wind up in prison" like him. He was always trying to protect me with his advice; it was up to me to heed it. And of course, me being young, most of what he said went in one ear and out the other one. My mom was out of the picture, and my grandparents did their best, trying to keep me from hanging around the wrong people. But when I turned sixteen, I ran away.

I never went to visit my dad again. Life moved so fast after that. I got a drug charge at seventeen for selling to an undercover cop at school. I was put on intensive probation plus two hundred hours of community service. I manned up and did it for almost four months, but then I slipped and failed a drug test. It was either go on the run or do the time for violating. I went on the run. It was the biggest mistake I ever made in my life.

I was tried and convicted of first-degree capital murder of a police officer. Same as my dad. I got a death sentence, but he had gotten life. My dad reached out through letters, and we got back in contact. The whole time I've been locked up, he's been there for me. Even after I wasn't there for him. Locked up or not, that's a father.

The few family visits I get are different than the ones I had with my father. There are no hugs, no pictures, no sharing snacks. My visits are only muffled conversations through a paint-clogged vent. There's no contact. It's very discouraging for both sides. I don't blame them for not visiting. If I didn't get to hug my dad on our visits growing up, I probably wouldn't have visited that much either.

Good news is, after thirty years of being locked up, my dad is getting out of prison. Now, whenever I have the chance to communicate with him, I find myself giving him the same advice he gave me so long ago. "Be careful and stay out of trouble." It's crazy how this world works. Now he'll be free, and I'll be the one locked up. Will he get caught up in his life and forget about me like I did him?

He won't be able to visit, because he'll be out on parole, and no one on parole can visit a prison. I just hope he writes a letter or allows me to call him, because I need my dad now more than ever.

73

I Knew What Was Coming

My nephew actually thought this here was my job. One day he asked his mother, "How come Uncle El doesn't ever leave work?"

But my son grew up knowing I was incarcerated. He didn't really comprehend what that meant, but really, how could he?

All his friends had fathers in prison. So he didn't think too much about it till he was around nine years old, when a few of them chose to go to the library and use the computers. While they were there, the boys decided to pull up their fathers' release dates.

I didn't have one.

When my son got home, he was in tears. "How come you didn't tell me my dad was never coming home?"

His mother figured the truth should come from me, so she made plans for him to travel across the country to visit.

I was pretty keyed up. I had no idea what to expect. But once the door opened and that oversized denim shirt and khaki pants appeared, all my reservations vanished. He sat down across from me. As soon as I saw those big, brown, ten-year-old eyes looking up at me through the plexiglass and bars, I knew what was coming.

"When you gettin' out?"

Such a simple question. Such an impossible answer.

I told him the truth. I didn't know. "But I can promise you I won't stop fightin'."

Three hours is nothing when you've got just this one chance with your son. But I wasn't gonna front. I told him I didn't have a release date because I was locked up for murder.

He paused. "So, you killed somebody?"

I paused, too. "No. I didn't. But you need to hear how being a 'playa' can still kill you." I ran down the particulars like a history lesson. Tears welled up in his eyes.

I winked at him. "Uh-oh, you cry like your dad. That's gonna be a pain in the ass when you get older."

He laughed.

I braced myself. He needed to know the rest. "Son, I'm fightin' a death sentence."

His little face went from confusion to shock to hurt. I explained that fighting my execution was an uphill battle, and I was gonna need his help.

He pushed his round face close to the plexiglass and said, "Whatchu need me to do, Dad?"

That was an amazing moment.

I leaned in, too. "You gotta ask God to give me the strength to keep fightin'. 'Cause I need to be out there with you."

He nodded. And then he said, "I love you, Dad."

That there in front of me was all the inspiration I was ever gonna need to keep me pushing through this dark hole of an existence.

74

The Real Question

I'm so excited; I've been looking forward to this visit for months. I'm showered and freshly scrubbed and dressed in my cleanest, brightest State-issue clothing. My teeth are brushed.

It's the first and possibly only visit I'll get this year, as I have no family in this state. I'm a little nervous. Those of us who have visits are called out and searched. Why? I have no idea. We won't have any physical contact with our family. We'll be locked inside of a four-by-five-foot booth separated from each other by barred plexiglass. The shakedowns serve no purpose, except, I suppose, to reinforce our subordinate position.

I'm locked into my booth. I've never liked tight, closed-in spaces. I start to become antsy. I try to think positive thoughts. I say a silent prayer for my family's safety; they've had to travel such a long distance. But negative thoughts creep in as I sit and wait.

There's a sudden commotion. I look up, and here they are. My sister, my daughter, and my granddaughter! My granddaughter, who's only two, hops up and bangs excitedly on the plexiglass, screaming, "Hey, Granddaddy, hey, Granddaddy!"

"Hey, baby," I coo dotingly. My goodness, she is so precious. It is my first time seeing her, and I'm filled with wonder. I smile so hard, my face hurts. I put my hand on the glass, and almost instinctively, she puts up her little hand facing mine.

My sister is talkative, as usual. I luxuriate in the sound of her voice. But I focus mostly on my granddaughter. She falls asleep in her mother's arms, and I stare, a soothing calm washing over me. My grandbaby.

When they leave, I feel elated to have seen them. Then I am sad. There's a perpetual melancholy here, and there's nothing to be done for it. I've tried everything: I've prayed, tried positive thinking, pretended indifference, played table games, listened to music, exercised to exhaustion—but nothing works for very long.

And then the real question surfaces: should I even allow them to bring that precious child to this dreadful, godforsaken place? She is so impressionable. I don't want her developing mind to think this macabre sideshow is normal.

I cannot hug her. I cannot hug my sister or even wipe away her tears. I can only watch helplessly. I am embarrassed to be in this position, but I never look away when emotions overwhelm us. I try to muster as much dignity as I can under the circumstances.

And how can I ask them not to visit, when just the sight of them soothes my soul? They're a part of me. I miss them terribly. But sitting there is more a reminder of our separateness than our closeness, the distance between us reinforced by concrete and steel and filthy plexiglass.

No one can see me now. I don't have to pretend everything is all right. No reason to posture, to appear strong. I simply allow the absurdity of the situation to be what it is, and I weep.

75

For My Heart Only

I was eight years into this bid when I was given a letter from my son. It was hand-delivered by my lawyer, who had recently flown across the country to interview my siblings in preparation for a new hearing.

I was stunned and amazed to receive the letter. My son must have learned something from my attorney that changed his feelings toward me. Maybe something about my own childhood. Because the last time my son and I had spoken, he was twelve, and I don't recall that talk going well.

He was my forgotten child. When he was conceived, I was thirteen. I was fourteen when he was born to his seventeen-year-old mother. We made an attempt at being a family, but really, what could a fourteen-year-old bring to the table? I did my best, but we didn't last a year together before his mother realized she needed an actual man in her life.

The letter from my son was humbling, raw with emotion. Although he reminded me that I had never really been there for him, he wanted me to know that from that day forward, he would always be there for me.

I've only spoken about this letter maybe four times in the past twenty-one years. And I won't really be sharing any quotes from it now. His words are mine, mine alone. They are for my heart only.

What I will share is the letter's profound effect on me. The love and affection he put into that letter broke me down to the second biggest cry and emotional breakdown I've known as an adult. And I never, absolutely never, knew what unconditional love was until that moment. Nor have I ever felt so unworthy.

I still bring the letter out, sometimes twice a year, and always on his birthday. I suspect I'll always cry, and my heart will always ache for the love lost to me. It's still hard for us to bond with three thousand miles and a lifetime of neglect now sautéed with guilt, embarrassment, and shame.

But I'm forever grateful and so deeply in love with the man he grew to be.

76

Guilty by Association

I still remember my first day on death row. I was stunned, but I managed to function. How I got from that first day to here, I can't honestly say. It's not something I allow my thoughts to entertain. Just making it through even one day here without becoming unhinged is an achievement in itself. Something to be grateful for.

We have to be strong, or appear to be, for ourselves and our moms. It's a mother's natural inclination to worry. It's already traumatic for them just having sons in prison, not to mention death row. We'll carry the stigma to our graves. It's a stain that marks our mothers, too. For me, that's the bitterest pill to swallow. My mom hasn't committed a crime in her entire life, but because of me, she sits in a prison, too, guilty by association.

When she visits, we sit in a cramped booth staring at each other through bars and glass permanently scarred, spattered with old paint, and smeared with the grime and oil from countless hands desperately trying to connect, as if love could be communicated by osmosis.

Sometimes my mother will say, "I can't see you, baby. There's a glare," and we'll adjust our seating, as best we can, to try to see each other better. She's so soft-spoken, I have to bend my ear to the screen to hear her. But I don't mind; I'd do anything to hear her voice. Conversations with her are comfortable and easy, as they've always been. But now they're also awkward, given the odd way we must communicate. I can see her. I can hear her. But I can't touch her. She's right there in front of me, but as far away as the moon.

I don't dare complain. Despite the discomfort, I wouldn't trade our visits for anything. I've heard the noncontact visits might be taken away and replaced with video visits. Who thinks up this stuff? I don't imagine anyone would travel hundreds of miles just to sit in a cold room and look at my image on a monitor. It is a pain to have to squint to see and to crane my neck to hear, but even that is preferable to seeing only a computer-generated image.

Sometimes when the visit ends, I get this sinking feeling, wondering if it's the last time I'll ever see my mom. I quickly shift my thoughts to other things. Maybe that's where the twenty years have gone, looking away from things that hurt too much to face. But now I face the reality that I may never again feel the warmth of her loving embrace.

I study her face during our visits. I love her laugh and her smile. She has the cautious optimism of a woman who's known disappointment and the quick grace of a woman who knows God. She possesses an authenticity that is rare and an ability to hear not only the things I say, but also the things I don't. She has the most amazing gift to make the most dire circumstances seem not so bad.

I'm not so smart, but I know to cherish each and every moment with her.

77

Pumping Iron

Hitting bottom is the realization that your life can't get any worse. For me, rebellion, drugs and alcohol, homelessness, mental hospitals, arrest for murder, suicide attempts, and death row were certainly dire circumstances, but they weren't enough to open my eyes. Maybe it's because I was a hardheaded teen, but what teenager isn't?

I had been on death row for three years when my youngest sister came to visit. She was thirteen when I ran away, and she now sat before me, a sophomore in college. Gone were her ponytails and braces or any tendency to beam at her older brother. Here was this shy young woman with very little to say to the man on death row.

Except this explanation: "Dad said to pretend you died. So, we do."

It was the last time we spoke.

Her words tore open my heart to expose every fault and poor decision I ever made. It was easier for people to move on with life rather than complicate it with mine. I understood. Still, I couldn't help feeling bitter that my siblings found ejecting me so easy. In that moment, there was nowhere to escape from my overwhelming sense of responsibility.

Failure was a natural part of my life. Success unnatural. But I knew nothing would get better until I tried to change. Finally, the single most important element in my recovery had arrived: I was sick and tired of failing and suffering for my stupidity. It was time for something different.

Maybe such a turnaround seems pointless or foolish, considering I might be executed in the years to come, but the future is only as relevant as it needs to be. Why come to death row to die when I could finally learn how to live?

However much time remained to me, I would show my family and whoever else cared to witness that I was more than a series of poor choices, more than just a red jumpsuit and OPUS number. Even if nobody else cared, I had to prove to myself that change was possible.

The first step was learning how to respect my body as the only vehicle I had to take me where I wanted to go. This meant stopping any self-abuse. The things I needed to do to take care of myself were embarrassingly simple: stop abusing drugs, stop harming myself, and exercise.

None of it happened overnight. Poor self-esteem clung to my thoughts, crawling beneath my skin, begging to be released through self-mutilation. A cigarette was always there as a quick vent, though each inhalation brought pain and blood, and every exhalation defeat.

Slowly, through calisthenics and weight lifting, my body grew stronger. Exercise became my meditation. Weight lifting taught me not to dwell on accomplishments or setbacks, but to use them to push for greater goals as the old ones fell away.

What I came to understand is that the simple logic of pumping iron is applicable to life in general: you set goals, work hard to achieve them, never give up when things get difficult, and use that success as motivation to meet greater heights.

The other step has been the longest and most involved: pumping mental iron. Books—hundreds of them—showed me exactly how little I knew. Learning could be discouraging or frightening at times, but along the way, a lot of things started making sense. I no longer allowed ignorance and failure to prevent me from becoming a better man.

This effort has helped redefine the way I live. Though I remain incarcerated on death row and the time is arduous, there is no doubt in my mind that I'm capable of putting behind me the boy I used to be and growing into the best man I can become.

78

I Became Him

I had no idea how her story would affect me. A mother, who had lost her son to an act of violence, coming to address a group of convicted murderers? I expected a rebuke. Maybe to be spit on. I expected cursing and yelling and a mountain of pent-up rage to come thundering down on my head as she described detail by detail how some lowlife scum just like me had murdered her son.

I expected to be left unsympathetic. Not uncaring, but incapable of feeling what she experienced, because my sympathies had been shaped by what it's like to be on the other side of the relationship. Although I had always felt a deep sense of guilt for the wrongs I had done, when I felt the anger of those I harmed, I shut down my compassion. It even hindered my remorse. In the face of hate, we tend to hate back.

However, as she described her experience, something unexpected happened. I suddenly became her son. It was *my* mother talking about *me*. I could see my mother's excitement and unbridled joy as she found me laying on her couch after being away from home for nine months.

I could see her tiptoeing down the stairs trying to be quiet as she mouthed the words, "He's here!" I felt my cheek move as I tried not to smile while pretending to still be asleep. I saw my mom's face as she realized I was awake.

It was me taking those pictures with my mom that day, taking her to lunch, telling her I loved her at least five times. I could see my mom's appreciation as I said she was beautiful.

I could see myself walking out of the house, anticipating fun with my friends. Never thinking that this would be the last time my mom would see me alive.

My own mother has memories as well, memories of my final days home. She, too, got one of those phone calls, and she cried and made noises that I am sure no human is supposed to make. But her son is still alive, even if he is scheduled to be executed. What if she was on the victim's end of that phone call, and I was the one who had been murdered?

I also have a brother. How would he have reacted to my funeral? Would he have gone into a manic phase? Would my mother have the ability and strength left in her soul to console him? And all this because of what? A few words? Or in my case, a few lousy dollars or some misguided principles?

It tore my heart to realize I had caused a mother to hurt like that. And I am forever grateful to have heard her story.

79

Definitely Christmas

Prison isn't the place where you want to be known as a warm and giving individual. At least, that's what I figured.

We had just finished one of the two edible meals we received each year, one at Thanksgiving and the other at Christmas. The atmosphere was different than usual, with steak and good spirits livening up the chow hall. But before long, the meal was over, and all the death row jumpsuits headed down the tunnel.

My spirits declined fast. It was my fourth Christmas without family. The closer we got to our block, the more helpless and the less human I felt. Three friends had already been killed this Christmas season, with more to come.

But then Hallmark, the cat who made all the greeting cards on the unit, asked a couple of us to block the officer's view. As we did so, he removed some of the holiday cheer from an artificial Christmas tree standing in the hall, a tree that seemed to taunt us with its plastic goodwill. I mean, how happy can you be while anticipating the upcoming executions of friends?

Back on the block, Hallmark rounded up construction paper, glue, tape, and straws, and together we produced the very first death row Christmas tree! Complete with a little help from the officially sanctioned corridor tree. It was historic!

We stood there admiring this symbol of our unity, not caring that it looked suspiciously like Charlie Brown's Christmas tree, only smaller. Then one of the guys said, "What about the star?"

Hallmark disappeared and returned quickly with more construction paper and a folded piece of paper containing glitter.

"Man, where'd you get glitter?" we asked.

Hallmark grinned. "Scraped it off other guys' cards last year. Been saving it ever since."

Just then, an older cat instructed everyone to look out their cell windows.

A line of people stood outside—yelling, waving, and holding a sign that read: MERRY CHRISTMAS.

Here I was, struggling to maintain my sense of humanity, and complete strangers that didn't even know my name were out there reminding me of it.

This place would never be home. But it was definitely Christmas.

80

Sidekick for Life

In prison, *friend* isn't a word we throw around loosely. But Big Bo wasn't just my friend; I called him my sidekick.

I dubbed him Big Bo because he always felt like the low man on the totem pole—the guy nobody looked up to or respected. So calling him Big Bo was my way of telling him he was significant, that he was my peer.

Sometimes he would tease me if I asked him his opinion about something and it later turned out to be wrong. He'd say, "It's your own fault! What you listen to me for? You're the Hero, I'm just the Sidekick!" And then he'd shoot me that toothy grin.

He was proud to be my sidekick. So proud that sometimes when he annoyed me, I'd joke that he was "fired."

He'd say, "You can't fire me, I'm the Sidekick, and a sidekick's for life. You must didn't read the fine print!"

"For life" really meant something to Bo, because he never had anyone in his life for long. He didn't know his parents all that well. Mostly he remembered how they used to put him and his brother through windows so they could open the door and the parents could steal whatever they wanted. The parents went to prison when he was still little, so him and his brother were in and out of foster homes until the State decided to give them to their grandmother. Then she gave them to the orphanage.

The orphanage wasn't much of a home either. They split up Bo and his brother, the only family he'd ever really known, so Bo was pretty angry over that. And some older boys who lived next door would force him to do things he didn't want to do, sexual things. So Bo ended up staying out for days and just roaming the streets to get away from the abuse.

His lawyers had argued that his IQ scores proved that he was retarded. Anytime I criticized him for something, he'd look at me with that goofy smile and say, "Well, you know I'm retarded."

Bo loved to play Scrabble and dominoes. I'll never forget the time he beat me: he told everybody that I had been "retardilized." Then he'd kid me, "How's it feel to be beaten by a retarded man?!"

One year, I was coaching in the annual basketball tournament and picked Big Bo for our team. I even drew up a play where he could shoot the game winner. When he got the ball, someone came running to block him, and he just closed his eyes, turned his head, and threw the ball. Needless to say, it was nowhere close.

We lost the game, and I teased him about that for days. And then, what do you know? He scored a career high the next game. Twenty-two points. I was so proud of him! I told him so. He was pretty proud of himself, too.

But the thing he was most proud of was his daughter. She meant more to him than anything else in the world. He had only held her once, in the courtroom, when she was a baby. She grabbed his beard and wouldn't let go. That was one of the high points of his life.

When he was sent to death watch, he had a visit from her for the first time. After seeing his daughter, he said he was ready to die.

Bo taught me a lot. Once, when I berated him for running errands for everyone all day, he said, "I like being a servant. I like helping people. It makes me feel important."

Where I saw nothing but people bossing him around and using him, Bo saw himself as a helper. He said, "If I was strong like you, I wouldn't stand for a lot of stuff. But people have rough lives, and they deal with it best they can. I think that's why God put weak people like me in the world—to make those guys feel stronger."

Bo taught me to have the courage to admit my weaknesses. To have compassion even for those that mistreat me, and to develop a true spirit of service.

I said, "You ain't weak. You're stronger than anybody here. You're the Hero, not me."

But Big Bo wasn't having any of it. "Naw, I'm the Sidekick. Sidekick for life! Check the fine print!"

81

The Huggy Boys

"You are not here to be rehabilitated," the man in front of us stated. The armpits of his charcoal suit were oily black with sweat. "I repeat, you are NOT here to be rehabilitated."

As if we hadn't heard him the first three times.

Whenever we requested educational opportunities such as GED programs—since most of the men here never graduated high school—we were met with the same refrain: "You are not here to be rehabilitated."

True enough. We were there to die. But until that final point, transformation was possible. And it was clear that if we wanted to feel and act more humanely, it was up to us. I think that's where the handshaking comes in.

This is a strange trait of death row culture: we shake hands. A LOT. We're mostly stuck on our pods, so our social interactions throughout the day are pretty limited except when we go to meals, religious services, or rec. Then we interact for a few minutes with men from other pods, which is when all the handshaking takes place.

As members stream into a church service, every one of us shakes hands with everyone else, weaving in and out. "Peace and blessings." "God bless you." "Peace, brother." From above, it must look like some intricate choreography. It's the same when we leave. To call it excessive is an understatement.

If my pod is lined up against the wall for commissary and someone from another pod happens by on the way back from an appointment, he'll likely acknowledge all of us with a nod. It's a way of saying, *You are not invisible*. Then he may greet some of us individually—fist-bumping one, shaking hands with another, pulling the handclasp into a half hug with the next.

Seeing this scene as our pods split after chow, one officer dubbed death row "the Huggy Boys."

Fine. There are worse names we could be called. We live together, sometimes for twenty or thirty years. We eat together, pray together, elbow each other's teeth out on the basketball court, borrow each other's books, teach each other to read, draw, play chess, write poetry. When one of us dies, it's like losing a limb. We are, unexpectedly, friends.

We are the Huggy Boys. Not here to be rehabilitated, maybe, but doing what we can ourselves.

82

Cellar Dwellers

Our death row basketball league season was pretty terrible. Known as the Nubians, we were 4–9 on the season. Everyone, including us, were pretty sure we'd lose in the first round of the playoffs. Not because we were incompetent, but because we struggled to function as a team.

One game, we were up seven points on the number one Dream Team when their point guard pushed one of our guys in the back. The refs only caught our guy's retaliation and called a foul.

"How you gonna call that bullshit on me? That shit's crazy! Who the fuck paid you off?" Our guy continued to melt down, hollering and getting in the ref's face, a man who was easily twice his size and doing time for two murders. During the tantrum, the Dream Team scored enough to regain the lead and eventually win the game.

His outburst had the rest of us yelling at him to get his head out of his ass and in the game, and when that didn't work, we begged Coach to bench him before Coach, screaming obscenities from the sidelines, drew a technical foul. The other starters looked at the bench warmers as if they would happily trade places. After that game, we earned a new nickname: the Cellar Dwellers.

I'm not much of a ball player. Good defense and hustle, but that's about it. I only started playing when the free weights on the yard were confiscated after two guys got into a fight and one used a dumbbell as a weapon.

It was the first such incident to occur in more than seventeen years. The guys made up soon after, but we never got the weights back. Go figure.

Lifting weights and playing basketball were not what was on my mind when a judge said, "This court hereby sentences you to death," but there were a lot of things I didn't think of back then, a month after my twenty-first birthday. How was a skinny white kid like me going to survive a violent world where seasoned predators and gangs ruled? Never mind that I sat chained hand and foot after being sentenced to death for a double murder. I didn't feel like a monster, just really confused by the trial, afraid, lost, and utterly alone.

The trauma of arriving on death row was obscured by immaturity, ignorance, and a heavy dose of psych meds. Most of the time, I read fantasy novels to escape or watched sitcoms on the TV. But then one of the guys got me lifting weights twice a week. Another had me doing calisthenics. And now here I was, playing in a death row basketball tournament.

The chatter was how the Dream Team would use the Cellar Dwellers for warm-up before going on to beat the other teams and win the tournament. Their point guard, Phenom, the best baller on the row, averaged half of his team's score by himself.

Within minutes of the first quarter, it became obvious we were a different team. The Cellar Dwellers communicated and played together, smothering Phenom with double teams and traps. By the end of the third period, we had a fifteen-point lead on the team expected to win the tournament. The watching crowd couldn't believe it. The Dream Team attempted a last-minute comeback, but it wasn't enough. The Cellar Dwellers won.

We played the Blazers next, a fast and savvy team who took an early lead. After some bad calls, Coach raved on the sidelines about bribes, which almost earned him a tech. But we took the lead with a minute left. On the bench, we prepared for another heartbreaking loss at the buzzer. But we made it to the championship round!

My brothers, the ones who wear the same prison garb as I, are a family of a different sort. We are all flawed human beings who have earned ostracism and incarceration. There are some who should never leave prison, but many more deserve a chance to prove they are worthy of life and freedom. Death and horrible circumstances may bind us, but humanity is how we share life with the rest of society—our ability to learn, love, empathize, regret, and make mistakes.

All we needed to do was win one game in the championship round. It would be the first such upset in the fourteen-year history of the "Ball Till We Fall" tournament. Excited from back-to-back playoff wins, our starters talked a lot of trash to the opposing team. They were so confident, they didn't even bother to practice or make plans for the final game.

But Team Dog Pound's coach really wanted to win. He watched all the games, took notes, and held strategy meetings with his players. Game day arrived two weeks late after several rain delays.

We were not ready. The wait had stolen the energy from our previous wins. The starters were sluggish and indifferent, mouthing meaningless reassurances to one another about winning. Frustrated and fouled, our captain struggled to keep it together but finally broke on his team. "Pass the damn ball! Don't worry about who's guarding me!"

Another player threw his hands up—"I can't play under these conditions!"—and walked off the court.

Team Dog Pound stole the ball and scored.

"What the hell is wrong with you people?" our coach Ayatollah fumed on the bench. "We're a team! We came all this way and you wanna give up?! Play some dang defense!"

It wasn't enough. We lost because the other team was better at preparation and teamwork. We lost because underlying all of our problems was a lack of knowing how to fix what needed to be fixed.

And yes, that is certainly a metaphor for our lives. But however flawed we may be, however much the world would prefer to forget about us, there is a simple truth that cannot be ignored, walled off, or executed. It is our ever-present desire to be both flawed and still recognized as human. This is what we cellar dwellers share with one another.

83

Your Neighbor

It started as a rumor. This beefy white guy wearing a too-small gray T-shirt and faded black nylon shorts—our approved casual attire—lumbered toward me. He came bearing bad news and seemed pretty happy about that.

"Looks like we ain't gonna be able to use the faucet in the closet for hot water no more. You know some guys gonna die without their morning coffee."

I cut him off. Enough already. What had happened?

"That dude J-Roc killed hisself—well, hung his neck in the closet, anyhow. Don't know if he actually died or not. Now, don't get me wrong," he grinned, "I get how come somebody'd wanna hit the ejection switch. But why make it harder on the rest of us, right? That's some selfish shit right there."

Apparently, during the investigation into the incident, someone uncovered a rule stating the closets were only to be accessible between 7:00 and 9:00 a.m. Before that, the closet and its contents—brooms, mops, and, most importantly, hot water—had been left open to us 24/7. No longer.

You could feel the resentment, irritation, and frustration gathering like pent-up static energy. No hot water meant instant coffee made with room-temperature water in our cells. Since there are only enough supplies for two men at a time to clean their rooms, two hours of closet access meant only a few of us would be able to clean our rooms each day. Our informal schedule of cleaning, based on access from 7:00 a.m. to 11:00 p.m., was shot.

When a rock is dropped into water, it instantly ripples the surface, and these were the surface issues. But it also continues disrupting the deepest parts. Petty arguments erupted over nothing and everything. We were more aggressive during our already rough basketball and volleyball matches. We exercised to exhaustion. We woke in the middle of the night to crank out five hundred push-ups, sit-ups, squats. We did wind sprints outside, running from an invisible enemy. Sad figures moped, dragged their feet.

I saw four or five men crowded around the sergeant's office asking whether J-Roc was going to be OK. The sergeant told them to calm down, that he had survived but was being sent to Mental Health. Everyone walked off, shaking their heads. We knew what happened on Mental Health.

It took me years to come to terms with my own death sentence. At first, I buried my eyes in TV, hid them between the pages of stacks of books, or withdrew into myself, pulling a blanket of medications over my head to keep the Monster out of sight. To me, I was already dead, my body just didn't know it yet. Suicidal thoughts came with the territory. Everything else, it seemed, was taken from me; I could at least still decide my time and method of death.

Even before my trial, I had attempted suicide, slitting my throat and wrists. I remembered Mental Health all too well, could see myself, naked and shivering, in an empty cell with nothing but my demons and a camera perched over the door to record these humiliations and document my mental deterioration. I had to see a battery of psychiatrists every day to earn a scrap of clothing. On Day 3, I got underwear. Day 4 was socks. Day 5, I received a T-shirt. It took more than a week to get dressed, much longer to regain any sense of dignity. I suppose these degradations were intended to deter future attempts. Well, I had decided that if there was a next time, I would sure as hell succeed.

For years, I hung by a thread. I wanted and needed to talk to someone about it, but how could I? Suicide was considered a sign of weakness and instability. Well, I definitely felt weak and unstable. The risk of failure was high—there's no easy way to die in here—and the cost of yet another failure was too expensive. I couldn't afford to jeopardize my escape route by confiding in someone only to have it spread to staff. Or if I changed my mind, I couldn't bear the social stigma that would follow me forever, the looks, the jokes. I was surrounded by people constantly but felt utterly isolated.

No, I couldn't talk about it. Nevertheless, suicidal thoughts glowed like red, flickering neon EXIT signs. When life got especially grim, I'd walk back there and sit beneath the sign. At least once a day, I'd review my escape routes to keep them fresh, just in case. I figured everyone secretly harbored the same suicidal thoughts and just kept quiet for the same reasons I did. I figured everyone's attitude was basically, "No blame, just don't cause harm to those you leave behind." At the time, I was convinced nobody truly cared about me personally, so I didn't have to worry about any harmful psychological consequences.

But now, looking at the effect of this attempted suicide on the others, I could see how wrong I had been. The men around me have become my family. They do care. When guys ask me if I'm doing OK and if I need anything, they mean it. They aren't just being polite.

I realized with curious shock that I couldn't remember the last time I had seriously considered suicide. Thousands and thousands of consecutive days I considered it, then nothing. What changed? For one thing, God gave me a sense of purpose. I took the focus off myself and stuck it to others. I allowed myself to care and be cared for. I quit being alone, aimless, hopeless.

I saw J-Roc through the plexiglass windows the other day when he returned from Mental Health. He was slouching near the back wall of the cafeteria while everyone else sat together at the tables. His posture bespoke overwhelming shame, isolation, defeat. I wanted to say, "I see you. I feel you. I don't judge you. I see myself when I look at you, and I don't consider you weak or unstable, only human."

I wanted to remind myself to never forget where you came from, what you've been through. I wanted to remind us all to open our eyes and look around, because strange as it may seem, loving your neighbor actually includes your neighbor.

84

Beyond the Wall

I came down off-balance from my rebound attempt, driving my ankle to the ground with an audible *pop*. Down I went, holding my quivering leg and inventing new ways to say the same profanity.

When the guard wheeled me into the prison ER, I expected to be told my ankle was broken, get some crutches and ibuprofen, and that would be it. But it was a Saturday with no X-ray technicians available, so the doctor gave me a pain pill and said I'd be going to an outside hospital.

A couple of guards muttered about the cost of an ambulance, while I stared at the splint, trying to keep my face neutral. Rattling in my head like a pair of carelessly tossed dice were two syllables—*out* and *side*. Over and over, through the haze of pain: *Outside. Outside. Outside.*

I hadn't been beyond the wall in seventeen years. My entire adult life had been spent in the same two hundred yards of dust and cement. It took more time to brush and floss my teeth than to walk to the chow hall, rec yard, or canteen. I'd become so accustomed to the lack of private space that my empty seven-by-nine-foot cell felt spacious.

Hands cuffed, chained at the waist, I sat on a gurney in the ambulance with my legs shackled over the temporary splint. To my left sat a transport officer, her hands gripping the neck of her bulletproof vest. Two more officers followed in a pursuit vehicle.

But I was too enthralled with the pavement slipping behind us to pay much attention to the officers. Too enthralled with the world. So much space! So many trees! So many leaves, green and glorious, branches shifting, swaying, waving. Engines hummed, a car honked, and I jumped, laughing madly at the sound. The officer looked at me until, wide-eyed, I couldn't keep the joy to myself.

"I haven't been out of that prison in seventeen years."

Even rundown houses with rusted oil tanks and peeling paint, overgrown weeds and shuttered windows, were perfect. Colors vibrated. My eyes jumped to cars I didn't recognize. They were real! Futuristic and fantastic. I knew I was grinning like an idiot, and I didn't care.

At the hospital, I was taken to a bed and X-rayed. Once the three nurses arrived, it was too crowded for them to work, so two officers stepped outside. The female transport officer and one nurse joked about what my foot would smell like in six weeks, what a pain in the ass showering would be, and told me to breathe as they moved my leg.

The banter died when a male nurse with an Eastern European accent asked what my red jumpsuit meant. An officer answered, "Death row."

Maybe it was the fresh air and vibrant colors that had hypnotized me into a false sense of well-being, but at the mention of death row, the noise came roaring back.

Nobody moved. Finally, a female nurse said, "Wow, that's incredibly sad." The male nurse looked away.

A familiar sense of shame and isolation washed over me. I wanted to leave the hospital right then. I wanted to escape their scrutiny. I wanted to be back inside where shame and isolation were the norm.

But wait, what had the nurse meant? Was it sad because they were wasting resources on a condemned man, or sad because their profession is about ministering to those in need rather than killing them? Maybe she actually saw me as a human being in need of care, rather than some sensationalized image of a monster.

She patted my leg and left. The male nurse was apologetic. "This will hurt. Push foot against my chest."

I did. The pain was intense.

"You know," he said, "no one ever put foot on me. You first."

I tried to smile as I pushed hard, breaking into a cold sweat. "That's good," I said, "not letting people put their feet on you. They might think you're a doormat."

He grinned as the material hardened around my ankle. "All done."

They wheeled me out of the hospital and into the warm night air. My eyes jumped from trees to cars to buildings and people and then locked on the vermillion brilliance of the setting sun. The light hurt, but I stared anyway as I struggled to inhale this achingly beautiful life on earth. For just a moment, I remembered another life, where I didn't drink from this world as if dying of thirst. Then the moment, and the sun, were gone.

85

Ten Cents a Minute

A phone call.

It's such a simple thing. But not so simple when you're only allowed one a year. Who gets those minutes—your mother, your grandmother, your kids, your wife? Sometimes the whole family would try and be together so everybody could hear my voice. But then something would go wrong, I couldn't call at the appointed time, and disappointment would be fierce. One year, after the officer on duty started making fun of me and imitating my tearful conversation, I swore never to call again. I never did.

For years, we'd heard rumors that phones were coming. I knew it was possible, and all the arguments for us having phones made sense. But the higher-ups don't believe in sense most times.

This time, however, the rumors proved true. Phones had been spotted. Not too long after, they installed one on our block. I was a little wary. We'd gone so long without access, I wasn't sure how I felt. Being cut off for so long had made me unsure. I was now more adaptable when things went wrong; I'd learned to prepare for and expect the worst.

I'm not sure when I started behaving this way. I was a scaredy little boy. There were certain sounds that filled my mind with impending doom. When *Perry Mason* came on the TV, the music made the hair on the back of my neck stand up. By the time the crescendo of dark piano notes filled our small apartment, I was already running, then airborne, diving into my mother's bed.

Or the song "Family Affair" by Sly and the Family Stone. His voice sounded like he'd just risen from a tomb. Whenever that song came on the radio, I'd run and find my mother.

"Boy, what's wrong with you?"

Just being near her, just hearing her voice made me feel safe.

I eventually grew out of those childhood fears, but I soon discovered other sounds that were even more frightening: "Freeze, police!" which anyone with a lick of sense knows actually means RUN. The sound of gunshots which can't be outrun. The clicking of handcuffs. Arrest is right; your whole life stops. Scratching your nose, tying your shoe, going home—simple actions are no longer possible. Those alien voices transmitted over the police radio, the flashing lights, being touched by unfamiliar, unfriendly hands, being taken to God knows where—it's enough to induce a heart attack, even in a kid. The one phone call allowed during the process may not seem like much, but it is a lifeline to a drowning boy. I always called Mom, and just hearing the soothing cadence of her voice was reassuring. It reminded me I belonged to someone.

Being on death row, I've long since gotten over the fear of being arrested, and even of being in prison. But I've never gotten used to not hearing my mom's voice.

Little Red was the first person on my block to make a phone call. He called his sister who he hadn't spoken to in years, a sister he always spoke about proudly, so I knew he loved her extremely.

I watched him nonchalantly from my perch at the rail in the front of my cell. The pod was hushed and almost noiseless; most men were in their rooms, asleep, reading, or just staring at the walls, so Little Red had the dayroom and the phone basically all to himself.

"Hey, Sis!" his voice thundered through the air space and bounced off the walls of the block.

He'd gotten through! Made a connection with someone who he'd only been able to call once every few years. Now he could talk to his beloved sister in the middle of the day during the first full week of June. No longer having to wait until some evening in December or somebody is sick in a hospital or dies.

Little Red twisted his body as he talked. I could see the glimmer of his glee beneath the surface of his skin. Although his countenance was somewhat stoic, macho, the ruddiness of his face betrayed his emotions and stirred up my own. This was a victory dance minus the footwork and drums. He waltzed away from that fifteen-minute phone call head high and back straight. And though I could see that his short legs were a little rubbery, he had a new pep in his step. Poppa got a brand new funk!

I made my first call last week. The operator said the process would take a few minutes; I would've waited all day.

Once I finally dialed the numbers, I was eager with anticipation, and when I heard her voice on the other end of the line, it was like I was back home again. She was eating something, "candy," she said. She always did that. She could be eating and still speak clearly and engagingly; it made her words sound yummy.

We didn't really talk about anything during that first call—we just talked. When the operator's voice cut in with the "You have sixty seconds remaining," I swear it was the fastest fourteen minutes of my life.

I said, "OK, I'd better go before we're cut off. Love you, too."

When I hung up, I was overcome with an emotion that felt brand new but was actually very old. The sound of her voice reminding me I belonged to someone.

86

You Can Do It

I had just left our Bible study when I noticed several men clustered around the chaplain. They weren't touching her, but they were pressing in threateningly. Her back was to the wall, and she was warding them off with sharp whispers and choppy gestures.

I decided to keep my head down and mind my own business.

I turned away and was halfway down the hallway when: "Jorge! Help me!"

Reluctantly, I slowed.

"JORGE!" I turned. The chaplain was hopping up and down, trying to see over the head of the tallest men. Reluctantly, I moved toward the guys, despite the warning in their eyes.

"What's up, Chaplain?" I asked.

A couple of the men peeled away, shaking their heads. The others fanned to either side.

A delicate, tragic sound emerged from the chaplain. "You have to help. It'll die if you don't."

I traced her gaze downward. At her feet, there was a small . . . cricket? And not just any cricket, a three-legged one.

I hate bugs. Maybe *hate* is too strong a word. How about *revile*?

The chaplain wasn't letting up. "Please. It won't hurt you."

Really? Then how come she wasn't catching it? The bug was right there at *her* feet, not mine.

"He's only got one hind leg," she pleaded. "You can do it, Jorge! How hard could it be?"

Well, as it turns out, pretty hard. The cricket's frantic bounce-bounce-bouncing was totally unpredictable due to his lopsided catapult system. After about a minute, I was sweating from squat-hopping around the hall trying to herd the cricket and pretty annoyed with the officer's amused grin, the chaplain's "Get him!" and the men's mocking "You can do it, Jorge!"

This was getting serious. I took a deep breath and spoke softly to the cricket. "You made a serious wrong turn to end up here, li'l fella. That was one heck of a bad decision. But I'm trying to set you free."

Within seconds, I had him cupped between my hands. Success! I could feel him ricocheting wildly off the walls of my palms. I bumped the rec yard door, but it was locked.

The officer yelled, "Are you out of your mind?! You can't just open that door. There are gun towers watching! You could be killed!"

Now, we both knew the gun towers wouldn't have noticed a door cracked open for half a second to release an insect, but he stomped off, saying, "And I'm not going through all that trouble just so you can save a damn bug."

Our spirits wilted. "Just set him by the door," the chaplain sighed. "Maybe he'll escape next time it opens."

"Sorry, li'l buddy," I said, gently setting him down. "I did what I could."

On my way down the hall, the chaplain called after me again. "Jorge, why did that happen?"

"What do you mean?"

"Why would God allow that to happen? Why would He move us to help a cricket, only to have a locked door defeat us?"

"Beats me," I said, thinking, *You're the chaplain* as I walked away. Then something occurred to me, and I stopped. "Maybe God wanted us to understand that He values the life of every creature. They're precious to Him, so they ought to be precious to us. I don't know, maybe success isn't determined by results, but by the heart. We did what we could, you know? The results are always up to God. Our hearts were in the right place. So maybe, in some way, we were successful after all."

87

The Kind That Never Go Away

"Something's up on the bridge."

The old man jerked his head toward the window where he stood smoking.

I answered from my bunk. "I just read an article about some really spectacular bridge somewhere they want to tear down but can't because the bridge is so well engineered and 'cause the paint is toxic. Nobody knows how to dismantle it or what to do with all the parts."

The old man hacked his choking cough. "This ain't construction. It's them people. In coats and hats."

"What are they doing?" I asked, not really caring.

"At the moment, jumping up and down to stay warm." His breath curled through the open arrow-slit window.

I shook my head. "Southerners." Winter always was an odd thing to witness in the South.

"They're singing," the old guy reported. "*We wish you a merry Christmas.* You feel merry, Yank?"

It was barely a month since the last execution. I still had that empty feeling in the pit of my stomach. The kind that never goes away. No, I wasn't feeling merry.

"How do we know they're singing to us?" I asked.

He shrugged. "You can hear it, so what's it matter?" he asked and lit another cigarette. "They come out in the freezing cold for somebody."

"Freezing?" I scoffed. "I don't think so."

"It's snowing. I seen some flakes."

I snorted. "Yeah, it's a damn blizzard."

"Ya might feel different if you was actually out there. When's the last time you was outside in the snow?"

I paused. I didn't want to think about that. About snow or Christmas, either one. The last card my mom had sent, maybe five years earlier, had a snowman on it. She said the snowman reminded her of the time at the Christmas carnival when I was three. I was wearing a blue snowsuit. Someone had dressed up like a huge snowman, and she said I ran right up and gave him a big hug. That's all she remembered, the enormous snowman and my little arms hugging him.

And then she wrote:

Listen to the quiet of the snow falling in your mind, the beauty of the night.

Imagine the fields and pine trees. O how beautiful . . .

Merry Christmas, my son.

I coughed and turned away. I hoped he thought the tears were from the raw wind. "Are those the same people who stand vigil with candles when they kill us?"

He let the smoke roll out his nose as he spoke. "Some. Also pen pals, friends, and family of guys here on the row. Church folks."

I watched the people in their winter coats and hats jumping and laughing and singing. I appreciated the effort it took to leave the comfort of their homes on Christmas Day to wish us a merry Christmas. Would I have done the same, year after year, execution after execution?

The old man grabbed his cane and shuffled toward his bunk. "Merry Christmas, Yank."

88

Making It Home

He was sentenced to life without parole in federal prison. I was sentenced to die. For more than twenty years, I've lived with the thought that I'll never see my brother again.

This is not to say I lived without hope, but there's a fine line between hope and wishful thinking. It was easier not to think about the very real possibility of never seeing him again, but it would take shape as I slept, leaving me in a cold sweat. I couldn't escape it even in my dreams.

His letters let me know he was still out there somewhere. He wrote about his appeals in the courts, which were summarily rejected. I wrote back my most encouraging words. But as his appeals were exhausted, his spirits deflated. His letters grew morbid. He began to question the purpose of a life that led to the dead end of a concrete cell. He began to question my optimistic way of thinking.

I stood my ground. If I relinquished my hope, I had nothing. He stopped writing.

I felt that loss like a part of my life ending. But I couldn't afford to trip; there were lots of people I was never going to see again. Still, moving on felt clunky. I imagine it was not unlike a war veteran learning to live without a limb. In a life that's felt a lot like a long tour of duty, I had learned that some things, although unbearable, simply must be borne. For the next few years, I just walked it off, albeit with a limp.

The only way he would ever leave prison was if the president granted clemency. The president was three months away from civilian life and granting clemency at a record pace. However, my brother's name remained absent from lists of prisoners being released, and time was running out.

Finally, he got the call: he was going home. As the news sunk in, I noticed I felt relief where there should've been euphoria. I realized I'd been bracing for the worst, a strategy developed through a lifetime of learning not to get my hopes up. More pain could always be withstood. Another heartache could not.

I called him.

"Ay, wassup, man. Yo, it's crazy out here, Slim. . . ." I didn't recognize his voice. I mean, I knew who it was, but it had been so long since I actually heard him talk that I didn't know what he sounded like. I knew his letter-writing "voice," and we'd exchanged photos over the years, so I knew how he looked. But it wasn't until our third phone conversation that I was reacquainted with his cadence and his candor.

Before coming home, he had to stay at a halfway house until he could secure a job.

The halfway house is in an area we both knew well; it's where we grew up. Nothing ever changes there, except to get worse. Even the name, Hope Villas, is ironic. The only things the denizens there can hope for is not to be beaten, robbed, raped, or killed before the next day. It's a peculiar location to house men transitioning back into society, with its high concentrations of poverty, crime, and hopelessness.

He came to visit. It was surreal, seeing my brother after twenty years.

"Man, I hate seeing you like this," he said. "We gotta get you outta here, Slim. Y'all don't got contact visits? This shit is crazy."

It amazed me that after serving twenty hard years in a federal penitentiary, even he was appalled at the conditions under which we had to visit.

I told him that while the conditions were bad, after so much time spent thinking I'd never see him again, I felt truly blessed and wanted to focus on the moment. I watched his animated expressions with delight. He always had a personality that filled a room, and the tiny visitation booth seemed hard-pressed to contain his energy.

He spoke passionately about not forgetting the men he left behind. I suggested he start an organization for the men and their families. He was in a unique position to speak to both sides. He then said he was at odds with his daughter. He didn't understand why she preferred talking on Facebook instead of talking directly to him. I suggested he be patient with her. She's not had her dad in her life for twenty years. That rift won't be bridged in only a few months; it's going to take years. No matter how much time has passed, though, that's still his baby.

He was accompanied by his wife. We've had our differences, and I've had some choice words for her over the years. She remembers every one of them. I opened the visit with a prayer. And an apology. After two decades apart, their relationship has been tried and tested, and they have endured.

I know he beat the odds. It's uncommon for anyone to walk away from life without parole, but my brother is an uncommon man. His strength, determination, and endurance are otherworldly. I hope he does start that organization. He has an amazing and inspiring story to tell. It's a story the world needs to hear.

Someone Was Going to Die

It was the moment of truth.
One way or another, someone was going to die.

I was in the middle of a heated argument when lockdown was called. As I headed to my cell, the other guy yelled some vicious remarks up at me. I'd never in my life felt so disrespected, and my first impulse was to stomp back and fight right then. But the officers were watching. As our cell doors slammed shut a few seconds later, I was in a total rage.

I had been raised in an abusive home where I was verbally and physically beaten daily. We lived in a violent neighborhood that tested my aggression just as often. I lived by the code of conduct of the streets, its violent system of justice, not because I wanted to, but because I had to in order to survive. I had never been to prison before, but as it turned out, street code and prison ethics were nearly identical. Every violation had a prescribed punishment. The guy I was arguing with had betrayed a friend to a snitch. I had caught him doing it, and in front of the guy, told our mutual friend about his betrayal.

In prison, street code is called the "Convict Code"—a list of dos and don'ts along with predetermined responses for offenses, like "snitches get stitches." This ethic is imposed on us from the moment we set foot in a prison. Despite my small frame, or perhaps because of it, I had a string of assault charges on my record beginning at age eleven and escalating from there, culminating in a double homicide that stemmed from an argument over a lesser disrespect than the one I'd just experienced. I knew what justice required of me.

However, I was also beginning to identify as a Christian. I had vowed to God, and myself, that I would not put my hands on another human being ever again unless it was self-defense or in defense of someone being victimized.

I felt like I was being ripped in two. The mental pain was excruciating. My identity as a convict demanded I hurt this guy as much as possible; he'd gone far above the type of disrespect that warranted a mere fight. I was outraged and righteously indignant. I was also afraid and humiliated. I was angry that he had put me in this predicament and that he would prey on my religious beliefs.

I felt ashamed and guilty for considering the deadly course of action, for so quickly reverting back to my violent mentality. But if I let it go and forgave, others would see me as weak. I'd be victimized and bullied.

My two identities warred within me, the opposing ideals trying to beat the crap out of each other, with my brain caught between. I went from knowing what to do, to being confused, to knowing I ought to do the opposite. I felt anger, fear, peace, joy, doubt, confidence, compassion, murderous indifference, mercy, wrath.

I had given my word, and your word being binding was a core value on which the entire convict code was built. But it was also a serious offense to break a vow to God. I must've looked like a madman in my cell, pacing, talking out loud, cussing, praying.

Then I clearly heard God say, "One of you has to die. Either you will choose *Me* and die to yourself, or you will choose *yourself* and die to Me."

I was desperate. "God, I can't let this go—I can't. The only way is if this guy comes and apologizes. But we both know as soon as those doors open, everyone's gonna be watching, and this guy's a bully who has never apologized to anyone."

Suddenly, a profound peace enveloped me. I spat in my hands and wiped the bottom of my shoes with them so my feet would have traction. I stretched and flexed my muscles and waited by the door, reminding myself to keep my mouth squeezed shut so I wouldn't bite off my tongue if I stepped into an uppercut. I didn't want to get hurt, but I was ready.

When the doors opened, I sensed God tell me to give Him sixty seconds. I counted them down. After ten seconds, the guy stepped in front of me. I backed into my cell. The adrenaline roared in my ears. I was a ball of coiled energy, ready to explode.

I could hear the silence of the pod listening, twenty pairs of eyes pretending to watch television, neck muscles bulging as they strained to keep their gazes pointed anywhere but at us.

Yet he made no move to enter. He stood there staring at his feet, his jaw working quietly as if rehearsing. Then he sputtered, "I, uh, I'm sorry for what I said. I was in the wrong, and I apologize. I want you to forgive me."

I stumbled backward and sat down hard on my bunk, convinced I had just witnessed a miracle. I also felt cheated and a little resentful because I knew what this meant—I had to forgive him. I had to wear the humiliation of the harsh words he'd screamed at me, deal with the social repercussions and challenges this presented.

I was also humbled, relieved, and grateful, because he was a bigger and stronger man than me: spiritually, he'd done the right but more difficult thing.

Forgiveness isn't about what the offender deserves; rather, it's a reflection of my character. That was the day I chose to be a Christian instead of a convict. Today, I am no longer the boy who entered this prison, but a man of God working to offer others the chance to change themselves and to recognize that the convict code of conduct doesn't write us. Unless we let it.

90

Sugar Rush

We watched them through the small holes that were our windows. For a long time, they watched back, suspicious. To them, we were wild things. Dangerous. Unpredictable.

It was Hoss, an old guy, who finally wore them down. At chow, he'd pocket some of his food and carry it to his room. Then he'd slide it through the window bars, calling, "Come on, baby. Got some nice eggs for you today."

And then, "Here, kitty, kitty, kitty."

Eventually, one let him scratch behind her ears. Then she came inside. He named her Sugar. Hoss never let Sugar down. One day it was chicken, the next tuna. The only things she wouldn't eat were the mystery meat patties. She'd carry those outside and bury 'em.

Free to roam the block, Sugar was treated like royalty, with respect and awe. When she wasn't scaring off mice and rats, she was curled up on Hoss's bunk, purring. Yet somehow she knew to scat when she heard the call "Man down!"

I stayed away from Sugar. When I was a kid, my cat Lilac used to sleep beside me. When I ran away from home, I abandoned her. I still felt guilty. I wasn't getting attached to anything ever again.

And then . . . something happened.

Everybody told Hoss he'd better cut back on the treats. Sugar was getting fat. One day, I heard the guys calling me to come look. No thanks.

Then I heard a tiny "Mew." And another tiny "Mew." "Mew." "Mew." Wait, what?! Kittens??!!!

OK, so maybe I did pet the little fur balls. And bring them milk. And yeah, OK, bathe them. We had no access to medicine for fleas, but we figured that if the state of our balding heads was any indication, the lye soap we used would kill most anything. In no time, whatever veneer of toughness or indifference I had cultivated in order to deal with the on-going executions basically crumbled. Their little kitten claws hooked deeper than the cloth of my red jumpsuit.

Some of the guards knew about the cats, of course. One of the female guards was like, "I ain't coming down this hall if those cats in here." But none of them tried to run off our furry friends.

Still, we all knew that much as we loved Sugar and the kittens, they didn't really belong there with us. The hardest day was when mainte-nance workers went through every unit and installed thick panes of plexiglass and metal grating over every cell window. You could hear Sugar and the kittens outside, crying.

Hoss couldn't stand it. "I'm sorry, baby," he kept saying. "I can't feed you. That window's gone. You got to find yourself another home. You can't stay with us no more. If you stay here, you'll die."

VIII

Every Day's Worth Celebrating

(FACING EXECUTION)

91

Deal the Cards

I was mad as hell about the outcome of my trial when I arrived on death row. It was this older cat, SC, who set me straight. He kept referring to me as "YOUNG" Buck. I thought he was sonnin' me, playing me like a kid in the death row hierarchy.

SC was shuffling a deck of cards when he said, "You gotta be able to deal with the cards you've been dealt before you can begin to change your circumstances. This is death row, li'l bruh. You ain't got a lot of time, so it's deal or die."

His grin revealed a rotten tooth as he flipped an ace, a queen, and back-to-back fives. "That's thirty-five," he said. "Let's get it in."

He dropped to the floor and commenced to doing push-ups. Now, I took pride in being an athlete, but that was a lot of push-ups. Still, I wasn't about to let this old-timer shine on me.

After a few sets, I was burning out and he was just getting started. He kept flipping those aces, kings, queens, and jacks as if they were a direct challenge to his will to live.

"You gotta deal with the cards, Young Buck."

Then he was given an execution date. He kept saying not to worry, that his attorneys said he wasn't going to be executed. They had missed a filing deadline, so the State's protocol was to give him a date.

I just thought, "Man, this guy is in serious denial."

SC came back from chow one day with the police beside him. A captain and two officers with a trash bag. Their job was to observe while he packed his stuff. The items that mattered to him he would put in a shipping bag to mail to his people. Or give them to a friend on the pod. Anything that wasn't to be mailed or given to a guy living here went in the trash bag.

He handed me an unopened pack of cards and an American Heritage dictionary, saying, "You can keep the cards, but when I come back, I want my dictionary."

I thought, "I can't believe this guy is still in denial." I figured his will to live was distorting his ability to see reality. But I said, "Sure." A dictionary is a prized possession in here.

SC was taken to death watch. He even ordered Chinese for his last meal. The State still has a protocol even if there's supposed to be a stay. And you know what? Even if everyone knows you're supposed to get a stay, if you're down there and that call doesn't come, they move forward with the killing.

But SC was right about his cards. And much as I needed that dictionary, I was happy to give it back when he returned.

Plus, we all ate some slammin' Chinese.

92

Weighing the Cost

When someone here gives you an item, it really means something. We aren't allowed to keep much. Books qualify as personal property, so no more than ten. Ten books ain't that much if you got a Bible and some study books for your faith. And then there's your appeal. It takes that many books to work on your case. So you find yourself weighing which matters more, your spiritual freedom or your physical one.

When I come across reference material I need, I free it from its binding. Once it's unbound, it's just paper, and there's no limit on that. So long as you can fit it in your six cubic feet of property. That's not much space for clothes, shoes, toiletries, canteen, books, and the other items someone would normally save.

I have one large manila envelope stuffed with yellowed pages scrawled by my dad just before he died (where he says if I'm found guilty, he's gonna shoot up the courtroom), cute drawings from nieces I've never met but still say I'm the world's best uncle, photos from friends and family. Everything else I read, reread, commit to memory best I can, and then tear to pieces.

You can see why we tend to be very picky about what we keep. When one of my neighbors got his date, he gave me his dictionary and a handball and said, when I needed to calm down, to just squeeze the ball.

I took the handball and on it wrote the date they executed him. Later, one of the sergeants accused me of writing gang numbers. But it wasn't some kind of gang thing. It was the date they murdered my friend.

Then the administration did away with the handball wall, so even though they'd given us the handballs, the balls became contraband. I didn't want to give mine up because it was a kind of memorial, you know. A memento. When the sergeant asked if the ball was contraband, I kept saying, "No, it can't be contraband 'cause you the ones gave it to us."

They'd throw me in the holding cage for an hour or more and then ask again. It became clear they weren't going to let me out till I said yes. Because once I said yes, it was contraband, and they could take it.

So faith, friends, your case, your freedom. You have to weigh the cost.

93

The Envelope

I was called down to the lieutenant's office.

After a long wait, in came the Warden and his cohorts: the Deputy and Associate Wardens. The Warden walked to his desk, retrieved a large envelope, and tossed it in my lap. Then he sat down across from me.

I opened the envelope. Inside was my execution notice. It was Monday, January 8.

I had less than a month to live.

I felt a surge of fear and rage and thought, "Let 'em do it!" Then I went numb. For a minute, two minutes, I couldn't hear anything. The Warden was talking, but all I could hear was white noise. Sounds. It was a long time before he came back into focus and I could understand what he was telling me.

At that point all I could say was, "That's the best way you could give me this news?" It wasn't clever, but it was honest.

I remember being totally in the moment. Crystal clear. In shock. My first thought was my mother and whether she was okay.

Then something came over me. A calmness. As I looked across the desk at this warden, I realized he was just as scared as I was. I could see a little sweat on his lip. I could see the jitteriness of his eyes. And it dawned on me that this man no more wanted to be in this spot than I did. The envelope allowed him to read aloud the information, as if the news were somehow less personal that way.

The Deputy Warden, on the other hand, looked like he wanted to tell me. Like he was somehow enjoying the process.

They asked if I wanted to make a phone call, and I said no. But the Warden suggested I call my attorney, which I did. She was flabbergasted at the short timeframe and faxed an official notice about this violation of the rules.

After two decades of being incarcerated, part of me felt this was all proper. It was time. With an execution date, I would have more access to my spiritual leader. More access to the canteen, to the doctor for meds. I would have access to phone calls. Possibly even access to my family.

But part of me wanted to fight. So we did.

The next twenty-one days were amazing to me. I walked out of that office with a new set of eyes. A new sense of hearing. A new sense of taste. Everything became so immediate. So important. Every conversation I had, I was so tuned in to this other person's point of view, I was so present to any need, to be of assistance, to add my opinion, to give whatever was needed in that moment.

Every step I took down the hallway for the next few days, for the next three weeks, I could feel my foot roll from heel to toe, I was so present—it was astounding. Every sandwich, every bite meant more. I understood what being in the moment, what mindfulness really was. I'm a practicing Buddhist, but I had never experienced this kind of presence before.

What it really meant was to be an ear to everybody else. Every conversation I had was so important. Guys that I had seen come in, grow up—twenty-year-olds who were now forty-year-olds. I'd seen them grow through all their pains; I'd helped them when I could; I'd given them what life information I had, to add to what they'd gained. They wanted to feel bad for me 'cause they knew I was about to die. And all I could do was feel for them, because I could see them struggling with the realization of their own mortality. It was really a beautiful exchange in humanity.

A few days prior to my date, I was sent to death watch. You stay there all day except for a fifteen-minute shower. They have guards stationed outside to make sure you don't harm yourself before they kill you. Sometimes you're allowed a contact visit with family. That's what I was counting on.

Sure enough, my mother came to say goodbye. And when she arrived, the chaplain informed her that my lawyers had managed to get a stay of execution. They actually managed to shut down the whole system here.

I was grateful for the stay. But I was also grateful for the experience of that month. I never grew so much in my life as in those few weeks.

94

Final Hours

Harold and I had exercised together for months. One day, we were midway through our routine when he was called to the Warden's office.

After he returned, all he said was, "They gave me a date."

We looked at our feet.

Two days before Harold's date, they came for him. The Deputy Warden, a captain, a lieutenant, and a sergeant, somber and resolute. This was strictly business, their faces said, nothing personal. Just carrying out a decision made by twelve of your peers.

Harold shed a stream of tears as he said his goodbyes but not much else. What more could he say? Or any of us? I shook his hand and told him he'd be missed.

Harold left with his head held high.

A few guys were quietly angry over his willingness to go peacefully; they couldn't understand why he smiled through his stream of tears. But sometimes that's what bravery means.

The rest of us? We just acted like Harold was going on a trip, a long one. Or moving away.

When you leave the block, you're escorted to death watch, a barren cell next to the execution chamber. That's where you spend your remaining hours. Final visits with your family. Final visit with your attorneys.

Then final preparations begin at midnight.

By then, the last supper is finished. Your clothes are stripped off, and you're given an adult diaper and a paper gown. The death watch guards walk you to the execution chamber. The viewing seats are filled with witnesses: an attorney, the prosecutors, the victim's family, a reporter.

You're strapped to the gurney, IVs hooked up. If the guards don't botch the chemical cocktail, it will take less than twenty minutes for you to die.

Back on the block, Harvey's final hours smothered our other thoughts. Card games were subdued. Sadness shaded conversation; anger and hatred for the State willing to trade murder for murder as if that were justice. There were discussions about whether a last-minute stay of execution might be granted because of some legal technicality, but it was the hope of a drunk with an empty bottle.

The air was clouded with more than cigarette smoke. A guy close to Harold heard someone laughing at a commercial.

"What the fuck are you laughing at?" The block went silent. "You think this is a funny place? Everything here a joke?"

That night, the block was intense, even with everyone in their cells. When staff stopped by for count, they didn't linger.

Around 8:00 p.m., the unit manager came and asked for calm. "This isn't the first execution most of you have been through, and it probably won't be the last. Anyone who needs to talk with the doctor or who needs a 'time out' in one of the holding cages, just let the sergeant know. And stay away from the windows."

The unit manager didn't want us seeing the protesters outside in case they found a way to communicate with or incite us.

Time crawled by. I wondered if it was the same for Harold or if time went too quickly. When he was denied clemency at 11:30, an officer was placed on each block to lend an additional sense of authority and control.

Once Harold was dead, the officers left.

After an execution, it takes several days for life to return to normal. For a while, the block is solemn, almost like a kind of hangover. There is quiet at meals. It's a show of respect. It's a small acknowledgment that we are not cows and pigs in a slaughterhouse. We are still men.

Cruel and Unusual

I was playing dominos when I saw them round the corner. The Warden, his assistants, and a handful of White Shirts. Only captains and lieutenants wore those, hence the nickname. They were the upper crust of this prison, and they had come for my neighbor.

The White Shirts entered our pod with an empty handcart, and the correctional officer in the control booth opened my neighbor's cell. I watched as they clustered around him, speaking quietly. His face remained blank as he put the last of his worldly belongings on the cart. This is when the rest of us started making our way toward him. It was time for last words, final daps and hugs. When he saw us, his mask of indifference started to crack. He attempted to turn away as the first guy bear-hugged him. But as he endured this onslaught of brotherly love, his eyes filled with tears.

When my turn came, I wanted to say something profound, but the look in his eyes was clear. *There's nothing you can do, because you can't even help yourself.*

I did the one thing I could. I gave him a hug and let the tears fall.

If you thought you could extend a friend's life for even a moment, what would you do? Would you defy the authorities? Would you suffer bodily harm? No matter the odds? How far would you go to protect the people you love?

And how many times would you have to face these questions before it became cruel and unusual?

Black and Mild

My first day on death row, this huge dude called Bass holds up the newspaper, and there's my face on the front page.

"You big time now, young blood," he says.

I figure his baritone's about to jump-start my first fight, and my stomach starts twisting into knots. Twenty pairs of eyes are watching me, and sweat beads are forming on my temples. This is my first time in prison. How am I supposed to respond?

But Bass just walks over and holds out his hand. We shake.

In that very first conversation, Bass tells me how he stabbed his son's mother while under the spell of crack cocaine. The man had so much remorse, so much regret. It brought my heart rate back to normal.

Bass was someone who always looked for the good in others. He had a positive impact on everyone around him. Through him, I started to see that even the best of us are flawed. I saw the inhumanity of rushing to judgment.

Even the staff recognized him as a leader. In the ten years he'd been in prison, Bass hadn't gotten one disciplinary charge. The officers said he was a model prisoner.

One day I was talking with another friend when he stopped and said, "Man, that sound right there? That's a bad sign. You know a man has lost it all when you hear him tearing up his trial transcripts. You know that's the end."

That's when I noticed it. Echoing through the block. Bass must have been shredding ten or fifteen sheets at a time. But the sound was also a sign that it was time to show our support. Neighbors came out of their rooms, all of us moving down the hall to rally around him.

A few afternoons later, me and Bass were standing at the dayroom window, sharing a Black and Mild cigar, when the chaplain appeared. Now, this particular chaplain only showed up when someone got their date. So he was known as the Angel of Death.

He looked at us and said, "What's the celebration?"

Before I could even exhale, Bass answered. "Chaplain, every day's worth celebrating when you're alive to see it."

Bass knew how hard his execution was going to be on everyone. Normally, we were only allowed to gather at chow or for religious services, and even there we have guards monitoring us. But they let Bass host a going-away party.

The dayroom was jammed with guys wanting to hear him speak. Bass thanked everyone for their love and support. He added, "Don't do anything stupid for my sake. I'm ready to go. Stay out of trouble and don't give the police a reason to make it harder on y'all." He knew how much we loved him and how easy it would be for a riot to start.

Then one by one, Bass said what he would miss about each of us. It was a testament to the respect, trust, and intimacy developed over the years of living in such a close environment. Bass was living proof that our sentences meant nothing if we really wanted to change.

The day Bass walked out of our block for the last time, a part of me went with him. I sat in my cell and cried. For the friend we lost. For the man the world would never know. But his death didn't change the education I received watching him live. Every day's worth celebrating when you're alive to see it.

97

Something Wasn't Right

Something wasn't right about me and my brother being accused of that crime.

It was night when they charged me. I was standing in the middle of this small room, surrounded by these men that kept shouting, "Didn't you kill that girl? You better tell us the truth!"

I could barely understand them, the words were coming so fast. I kept saying, "I'm telling the truth! I did not kill that girl!" I was crying and confused and scared. I just wanted to go home. I could hear my mother pleading with the detectives to let her see me. And they said, "If you don't keep quiet, we'll lock you up, too!"

Hours passed like this: one, two, three, midnight, four. I asked the investigator to please let me go home. He said he would if I just signed some paperwork. I was so relieved. It was two in the morning. I signed where they told me and got up to leave. On my way out the door, the officer stopped me and placed me under arrest. I started to realize the police had tricked me. I had made a terrible mistake. I signed my own life away for nothing!

The next morning, the police claimed I'd told them the people's names, the details about the crime scene, everything in those papers I signed. But I didn't tell them anything. They wrote it all.

When I heard the verdict, I fell out on the courtroom floor. Inside of me was mad and angry at these evil peoples for finding me and my brother guilty. I didn't believe this could happen. I was twenty years old and sentenced to die. My brother was fifteen. And we was both innocent of this crime.

Still, I never stopped believing I'd get my freedom, 'cause I didn't do no wrong to come to death row. I knew in my heart that one day I would go home to be with my family again. They never believed I was guilty.

But us getting sentenced to death destroyed them. Especially my mommy. She was never the same anymore when she lost her only two sons to death row. It tore her apart, and that broke my heart real bad. So I kept her in my prayers all the time. I never got to touch her again. When I lost her, it ripped me apart to where I didn't want to live anymore, but I had to be strong for my little brother.

That very first day, I had to start being a man and taking care of us. That first day, sitting on the bunk bed in a one-man cell with no one to talk to, I felt lost and empty inside my heart, and lonely, hurt, too. I knew there was a God, but I was so busy in the world, I did not have time for God. So right then, I did something I had never done before, and that is pray. I prayed for guidance, strength, and comfort to deal with that place. I couldn't do it on my own. I knew that God was the only one that could help me in a place like death row. And after I finished praying, I felt His presence right there in that isolation cell with me. I'd never experienced anything like it in my life before.

Let me tell you something, death row is no place for no one. It's a place of pain, loneliness, heartache, tears, troubles, depression, problems, and suffering. But what I never thought would exist is there were brothers on death row that was good peoples who wanted to help us. So I was well loved by a family on death row, too.

This place is hell, but at least we have each other. In 1986, I lost my first friend here. I didn't look at him like a killer. That man was like a brother to me. So we are a family here, but we are constantly waiting for the State to decide to take one of our "family members" away. Still, we try to keep their memories alive. We don't want to be as forgotten about in death as we were by people outside when we were still alive. Because we feel forgotten here.

It's innocent people on death row, and other cases that don't have innocence but still they don't deserve the death penalty. People change in prison. There are good men here. That's why it's wrong for the system to kill us and pretend they are carrying out justice. They're the ones committing murder.

I say for other innocent peoples on death row, stay strong with a fighting spirit. Don't never give up. Keep fighting to the end and keep your head up, 'cause help is on the way. I spent thirty years on death row as an innocent man, but tomorrow I walk out, free. I just thank God for choosing me to live on.

I would have missed so much otherwise.

Holy Week

Most of us know what's coming. We sit down and remove our shoes. Our socks are clean. So are our feet.

Some don't know, though, and that's pretty embarrassing for everyone. There's a CD playing, and we're encouraged to sing along, but, um, no.

The priest kneels in front of us, washes our feet, and anoints them with oil.

Frankly, most of us are relieved when it's over.

I suppose we're embarrassed that someone of a higher standing in the world is humbling himself before us. But there's something else. I realize that I'm considered to be the scum of the State. I've been condemned to death. And there's a part of me that's defiant over that label. This defiance is a shred of pride I cling to. But however small that pride may be, I'm shamed by it when the priest washes my feet.

Some guys skip the Holy Thursday Mass because it brings up too many uncomfortable feelings. But I go. It reminds me that even though I may think I'm at the bottom of society's barrel, Christ would serve the lowest of the low without hesitation. Seen through the eyes of Christ, there is no better or worse.

Dawn

The day I got my execution date, I learned something that's never left me. You have to be right here, in this moment. Like a child. They're not thinking about tomorrow or last week. They're just here. Now.

Seeing a smile on someone's face, the light in their eyes, is enough. That's perfect contentment. That's joy. It's taken me a lifetime to learn that life's deepest meaning isn't found in accomplishments, but in relationships.

All there ever is, is this moment.

You, me, all of us, right here, right now, this minute, that's love. And that . . .

That's a whole lifetime.

Afterword

TIMOTHY B. TYSON

On the bright Sunday afternoon of February 23, 2020, Ahmaud Arbery, a broad-shouldered, twenty-five-year-old Black man in shorts and running shoes, walked into a house under construction—with a roof but lacking walls—in Satilla Shores, a virtually all-white subdivision of Brunswick, Georgia. He had been there before; the neighborhood was close to where he lived with his mother, Wanda Cooper-Jones. A devoted athlete, Arbery jogged in Satilla Shores regularly, his father said.

The owner of the construction site, Larry English, lived a couple of hours from Satilla Shores. He had installed several security cameras at the site and received a text message anytime the cameras detected motion. On four or five occasions since late October 2019, the cameras had spied uninvited visitors, including an older white couple and some kids from the neighborhood who reportedly took some boards. English first called 911 at 10:04 p.m. on October 25 to report that a young Black man with tattoos had entered; later, he thought this man might have been Arbery, though the resemblance is not strong. On November 17, a white man and woman came into the house together, but English did not call 911. The following night, a young Black man walked on camera; English thought he resembled the young Black man who had come on October 25, twenty-three days earlier, but could not be sure. A neighbor, Diego Perez, texted English the next day: "If you catch someone on your cameras, let me know right away, I can respond in mere seconds."

A month later, on December 17, Ahmaud Arbery appeared on the security cameras. On no occasion had Arbery or the young Black man who may or may not have been Arbery taken or disturbed anything. English later said that the directions from which Arbery entered and left suggested that Arbery was getting water from a sink inside or one of two spigots outside.

English had used their non-emergency number to inform the Brunswick Police Department about some of the trespassing incidents, not including Arbery's last visit on February 23. According to his attorney, J. Elizabeth Graddy, English never used the word *burglary* to describe any of the incidents. In response to English's phone call on December 17, a member of the Glynn County Police Department texted English on December 20 about a former officer in the neighborhood, Greg McMichael, a sixty-four-year-old white man with a full white goatee. "Greg is retired Law Enforcement and also a Retired Investigator from the DA's office," the text read. "[McMichael] said please call him day or night when you get action on your camera."

"It appears," said Graddy, "that Gregory McMichael had been informally 'deputized' by the Glynn County Police Department." After seven years with the police department and then one year as an investigator for the Brunswick district attorney's office, Greg McMichael had retired from law enforcement a year earlier, though he was clearly still engaged with the law enforcement community. He lived in Satilla Shores, only a couple of blocks from his son, Travis McMichael, a stocky, red-faced thirty-four-year-old with a full reddish beard. According to English, he never even saw the current police officer's text and did not know either of the McMichaels.

Travis's house, however, stood only two doors down from English's construction site. On February 11, Travis called 911 to report that a Black man was trespassing on the site again. Apparently this visit did not set off the security camera alarm. It is unclear how Travis himself heard about the intruder, though he might have seen the Black man or another neighbor might have tipped him off; both Diego Perez and another watchful neighbor lived close enough to have noticed. The younger McMichael told police that he personally had not seen the man trespassing before. At first, Travis said, he had "just chased him," but he quickly turned back to wait in his truck for the police.

Another neighbor, speaking on condition of anonymity, told a reporter that he had seen Ahmaud Arbery in the front yard of the site at about

1:00 p.m. on February 23. From behind an oak tree, he said, he "called the police, [Arbery] saw me, and he ran away." The neighbor disputed that Arbery was jogging in Satilla Shores. "He wasn't out for a jog, put it like that," charged the neighbor. "You don't go jogging wearing saggy pants, saggy shorts," he said, referring to the hip-hop-inflected fashion popular with the young and unpopular with many older folks. The video shows Arbery in a T-shirt, running shoes, and knee-length, though not notably "saggy," shorts. Arbery left the site running at a jogging pace, said English's attorney, similar to his pace on the video taken by Arbery's pursuers a minute or two later. If Arbery was fleeing, he did so slowly and on a public road.

It is not clear how Travis McMichael became aware that a Black man had been at the construction site, but when he did, he called his father—and 911. "There's a guy in a house right now, it's a house under construction," Travis said, giving the address.

"And you say someone's breaking into it right now?" asked the 911 operator.

"No," replied Travis, "it's all open, it's under construction." His voice rose sharply. "And he's running right now, there he goes right now!"

"What is he doing?" the operator asked.

"He's running down the street," Travis said urgently.

"OK, that's fine, I'll get them out there," replied the operator. "I just need to know what he was doing wrong. Was he just on the premises and not supposed to be?"

"He's been caught on the camera a bunch before at night," said Travis. Responding to another question from the operator, he said, "A black guy in a white T-shirt. And he's done run back through the neighborhood!" Travis ended the call quickly.

Arming themselves with a shotgun and a pistol, the McMichaels jumped into Travis's white pickup truck to try to catch and confront Arbery. Emblazoned on the front of the truck was the Gadsden flag, a bright golden banner with a coiled rattlesnake over the inscription "Don't Tread on Me." The "rattlesnake flag" in recent decades had become the most common symbol among neo-Nazis, neo-Confederates, and far-right militias—the murderous right-wing mob in the lethal clashes in Charlottesville in 2017 marched under it—though others have sported the flag, too. With his shotgun across the seat, Travis drove the truck, and his father, carrying a .357 Magnum revolver, rode in the back.

As they pulled away, their friend and neighbor William "Roddie" Bryan was waiting in his truck with a video camera. With Bryan, Diego Perez, the anonymous neighbor, the two McMichaels, and perhaps others engaged, it seems clear that Satilla Shores harbored some kind of self-appointed white posse, though in some sense Greg McMichael had been illegally sanctioned by the police. "When I saw [the police department's texts to Larry English]," said attorney J. Elizabeth Graddy, "I immediately understood that an organization had been developing in that neighborhood since at least December." Roddie Bryan told agents from the Georgia Bureau of Investigation (GBI) that he had seen Ahmaud Arbery running in the neighborhood on several previous occasions and had tried to question him without success. A GBI investigator, Richard Dial, reported that a search of Roddie's cell phone and social media posts later revealed countless anti-Black statements and racial epithets.

If racial antipathy had not ushered Greg and Travis McMichael to take up weapons and stalk Ahmaud Arbery, it is unclear what did. The elder McMichael claimed later that Arbery looked like a suspect in two recent thefts on their street. About two months earlier, Greg McMichael had called the police to report that someone had stolen his son's Smith & Wesson 9 mm pistol from Travis's truck, which Greg had left unlocked. But since no one had witnessed any thefts, it is unclear how Greg knew what a suspect in the alleged crimes would look like. It is possible that his contacts at the Glynn County Police Department had shared the footage from Larry English's security cameras; the anonymous neighbor down the street from English's construction site claimed to have seen security camera footage, and weeks later, Roddie Bryan brought GBI agents into his home and showed them what appeared to be the same footage. But none of the young Black men who appeared in that footage had stolen or damaged anything at the site. Larry English asserted that he had never had any contact whatsoever with Greg or Travis McMichael.

The McMichaels and Bryan leaped into their two trucks and found Arbery easily; there are only five streets in the neighborhood. Both vehicles tried to cut him off and force him to stop and face their demands. Unarmed, Arbery simply turned and jogged in the opposite direction. He had committed no crime, nor had the police suspected him of committing one. His only "suspicious" behavior was being Black and running through the neighborhood. The three white men who hunted Arbery possessed no authority save that which adheres to white men with fire-arms in America. When police or vigilantes kill unarmed Black men in America, there are generally no arrests, prosecutions, or convictions; rarely does anyone claim that these killings are morally right, simply that they are committed in self-defense or legal under various state "stand your ground" laws. Some killings spark protests and national controversy; others, often equally egregious, pass unnoticed. Anti-Black vigilantism, *New York Times* columnist Charles M. Blow wrote on May 6, 2020, "marks black masculinity as menacing, and state laws protect the vigilantes' rights to involve their weapons and their power to end lives."

The McMichaels wheeled the truck around and once again parked in the street ahead of the approaching jogger. In the other truck, Roddie Bryan cruised slowly behind Arbery, filming with his cell phone. Greg McMichael stood up in the back of Travis's truck and waited with the revolver. Travis jumped out of the front seat, shotgun at the ready, and moved to the left side of the street to block Arbery's path.

Greg called 911. "There's a black male running down the street," he told the operator, who asked what street in Satilla Shores they were on. "I don't know what street we are on," Greg replied. Turning to the scene before him, he then yelled to Arbery, "Damn it, stop!" And to his son, "Travis!" The operator tried to ask more questions, but there were only scrambled noises before the line fell silent.

As Arbery quickly ducked up the right side of the truck to elude Travis McMichael, Travis leveled his shotgun and dashed back to confront him. Bryan's video camera was blocked by the truck as the two men collided, but it caught them a second later as they careened back across the front of the truck and into the street. All the while, Arbery tried to push aside the barrel pointed into his chest or snatch it away. After two shotgun blasts, Arbery broke away and swayed two or three steps like a running back fighting to remain upright. The shotgun barked a third time, and the young man dropped to the pavement and bled to death.

Roddie Bryan told investigators that Travis stood over Arbery's body and yelled, "[Expletive] n-@@@@@!"

When Glynn County police officers arrived, they found Greg McMichael's hands covered with blood. They briefly interviewed their former colleague and then let the father and son return home. Later that day, a police investigator, relying solely upon McMichael's account, telephoned Wanda Cooper-Jones and explained that her son had committed a burglary and had been shot dead "by the homeowner."

Four days later, the Brunswick district attorney recused herself because of her relationship with her former investigator, Greg McMichael. The investigation then fell to DA George E. Barnhill of the Waycross, Georgia, Judicial Circuit, the second of four prosecutors. Barnhill kept Roddie Bryan's video to himself and quietly sat on the case for six weeks, filing no charges and offering no explanations. Barnhill instructed police not to arrest the McMichaels. On April 5, District Attorney Barnhill cited complaints "that my son works in the Brunswick District Attorney's office where Greg Mc-Michael retired some time ago" to justify his decision to recuse himself in a grudging letter he wrote to the Glynn County Police Department.

Barnhill's letter, however, went much further than his recusal. He blamed all the fuss over Arbery's killing on Wanda Cooper-Jones's "unfounded allegations of bias"—and, in a separate letter to the state attorney general, on another Black "rabble rouser." Barnhill described the killing as entirely legitimate under Georgia's citizen's arrest laws. The three white men "were following, in 'hot pursuit,' a burglary suspect, with solid first hand probable cause, in their neighborhood, and asking/telling him to stop." The white men had a legal right to carry their guns openly, he noted, although this well-known law was never at issue, nor does the right to bear arms include the right to shoot people with them. Barnhill made the dubious claim that the still-unreleased video proved that Travis McMichael merely exercised his right "to use deadly force to protect himself." He did not appear to reflect that a safer way for Travis to protect himself might have been to remain home, or at least to stay in the truck with his shotgun until the police arrived. It was telling that Barnhill's narrative of Arbery's death only began at the two seconds when the two men clashed in front of the truck, at which point, he claimed, it was merely a struggle over the weapon, which might well have ended in Travis's death had he not pulled the trigger.

He did not note that three white men without legal authority, without witnessing any crime, had seen a dark-skinned man jog past and concluded that he was a criminal menace. The McMichaels, at least, had armed themselves with guns, and the trio chased this Black man in two vehicles. The unarmed jogger did not flee, but merely turned away and continued his workout. The white men blocked the road twice and then killed him for failing to acknowledge their presumed authority over him.

District Attorney Barnhill insisted that the video clearly revealed that Arbery had attacked the white man, which it did not show at all; it did show Travis McMichael sprinting across the road with a shotgun leveled at Arbery. Barnhill went so far as to claim that "we do not know who caused the [shotgun] firings." Merely by jerking the barrel of the gun one eighth of an inch, he asserted, Arbery easily could have caused the shotgun blasts himself. Yes, he might well have shot himself—how can we know? "It is our conclusion," he insisted, "[that] there is insufficient probable cause to issue arrest warrants at this time."

On May 5, over ten weeks after Ahmaud Arbery's ostensible suicide, a local lawyer and gadfly, Alan Tucker, released Roddie Bryan's video of the killing—at the request, Tucker claimed, of Greg McMichael, who had mistakenly believed it would exonerate him and his son. When the video appeared online, millions of viewers differed sharply with Barnhill's description. On May 6, *Newsweek* observed that the video showed that Arbery had not instigated the fight. Instead, they noted, it showed him "trying to run past the truck before the confrontation began."

As for Barnhill's insistence that Georgia's citizen's arrest laws protected the men who killed Arbery, on May 8 the *Washington Post* quoted a former federal prosecutor: "This was a far cry from a lawful arrest, and the citizen's arrest defense is very likely meritless." He noted that the white men had not witnessed any crime, as required by the laws. "Arbery was unarmed, chased down, and then shot and killed," he said. "This sounds a lot more like murder than an arrest." The former prosecutor also observed that for a district attorney "to turn into a defense attorney on behalf of people who just shot an unarmed man in the street while he was jogging" was "inappropriate in every way."

Heartbroken, Wanda Cooper-Jones found some solace in the ghastly cell phone footage. At least, she said, it "proves that my son was not committing a crime. He was out for his daily jog and he was hunted down like an animal and killed." The 2020 Democratic candidate for president, former vice president Joe Biden, asserted that Ahmaud Arbery had been "lynched before our very eyes" and that "these vicious acts call to mind the darkest chapters of our history."

Seventy-five days after Arbery's murder—and three days after the video of the killing sparked global news stories and nationwide protests—yet a third prosecutor resigned, asking the GBI to take over the investigation.

In thirty-six hours, the GBI found "more than sufficient probable cause" to charge the men who took Arbery's life. The state attorney general named a fourth prosecutor, Joyette M. Holmes, to take the case. The first woman and the first African American to serve as district attorney in Cobb County, Holmes managed forty-five lawyers and an annual budget of $8.5 million—which meant welcome resources for the prosecution of this murder, which some called a lynching, and not without cause.

Lynching remains suspect language, however, because it has become one of the most misused terms in our language. Clarence Thomas, in his 1991 Senate confirmation for the U.S. Supreme Court, famously denounced allegations of sexual harassment against him as "a high-tech lynching." Seven years later, Senator Joe Biden and several other Democratic legislators compared Bill Clinton's impeachment to a lynching. When the House impeached Donald Trump in 2019, the president declared, "All Republicans must remember what they are witnessing here—a lynching!" In the wake of peaceful protests over the 2013 acquittal of the self-appointed security guard who killed Trayvon Martin, GOP pundit Newt Gingrich claimed that protesters intended, "basically, to be a lynch mob." In 2018, R. Kelly's public relations team called the boycott of his music in response to pedophilia and abuse charges a "public lynching." Meanwhile, Bill Cosby's defenders dug so deeply into demagoguery as to compare his multiple convictions for sexual assault to the notorious 1955 lynching of fourteen-year-old Emmett Till.

George Orwell, in his 1946 essay "Politics and the English Language," called this kind of nonsense "political language," words "designed to make lies sound truthful and murder respectable, and to give an appearance of solidity to pure wind." Gross injustice or extraordinary brutality does not automatically qualify a crime as a lynching. Nor does lynching require a rope or a killing committed in the public square. The accepted definition of lynching among scholars and anti-lynching activists since the 1930s is a murder committed by two or more people who believe themselves to be acting in the service of race, justice, tradition, or community values. If this does not strictly apply to what Greg and Travis McMichael did to Ahmaud Arbery, which I think it does, then surely it became an ex post facto lynching when virtually the entire local judicial establishment justified their actions and clearly intended not to prosecute them.

In this all-too-familiar story, still unfolding in 2020, we can see patterns discernible from the origins of the United States of America through the nineteenth and twentieth centuries—patterns that resonate today. We see white men policing white space and criminalizing Black bodies in order to preserve a hierarchy of racial caste. We see stark lines of race and place alongside the blurred lines of legal and extralegal violence. We see white skin as the badge of authority to destroy Black bodies. As in the heyday of lynching at the turn of the twentieth century, we witness the collaboration of local law enforcement and judicial systems to deny that a flagrant murder even constituted a crime. We see words and actions by which public officials make clear that any requirements of their oaths of office remain elective in cases involving darker-skinned citizens. Here we also observe one of the shopworn customs of white supremacy, wherein those same officials slander the victim to stamp official vindication on extralegal murder and to suggest to the public that the killing represented at least rough justice.

This is the intersection in America where social control, lynching, vengeance, and the death penalty first met at least 150 years ago, though white supremacy—the notion that the Creator made humanity in an inherent hierarchy of moral, cultural, and intellectual worth—was the driving engine. Christian concern for the souls of the enslaved had been the first rationale—as opposed to reason—for the enormous death machine of the Atlantic slave trade. Of course, staple crop agriculture with enslaved laborers was the petroleum of the seventeenth, eighteenth, and nineteenth centuries and constituted the actual reason. When some Africans began to convert to Christianity, the question arose as to whether they then became free. White supremacy, this notion in which darker-skinned persons are primitive, almost a separate and inferior species, unfit to govern themselves, and well suited to slave labor, became a rickety substitute for the religious rationale.

By now, white supremacy, social control, lynching, vengeance, and the death penalty have become like old married couples telling the same stories over and over, though, like many family narratives, they have evolved over time. White men created what we might call "The Black Beast Rapist and the Bruised Lily of White Womanhood," a politically driven Reconstruction-era confection that peaked in the late nineteenth and early twentieth centuries but lingers to this day. This oft-told tale served to justify mass murder, assassinations, racialized sexual assaults against Black women, mob violence, lynching, and massive electoral fraud, among other coercions necessary to block Black citizenship and interracial "Fusion" politics. "The closer a black man gets to a ballot box," a Black preacher joked, "the more he looks like a rapist."

This sleight of hand shifted the blame onto the victim, a trick that would remain convenient in maintaining the social structure of white supremacy, as well as its underlying notions of superiority and inferiority, and the need to police the color line with violence. The narrative, for example, that fourteen-year-old Emmett Till, a Black boy lynched in Mississippi in 1955, allegedly for sexually assaulting a white woman, should have minded his manners and thus had it coming, returned in 2012 as the tale that seventeen-year-old Trayvon Martin smoked marijuana and therefore must have somehow caused his own death at the hands of a self-appointed "security guard."

Nobody could ever calculate how many Black Americans have died "resisting arrest." But the count now includes George Floyd, whom white conservative commentators claim died of heart disease, high blood pressure, and drug abuse, and because he lived in a city run by liberals, among other things. The classic topper, put forward by Winnie Heartstrong, a candidate for the Republican nomination for the U.S. House of Representatives from Missouri: George Floyd did not die at all; instead, agitators staged his death to stir up racial trouble, and Floyd actually still lives in hiding. Sixty-five years earlier, Mississippi authorities made exactly the same claim about Emmett Till.

Since the casual killing of George Floyd on camera, we have witnessed unprecedented protests by a multiracial, multigenerational uprising whose power grows more poised and peaceful by the day, revealing a newly mobilized majority in our midst. Because of the protests, most Americans now support Black Lives Matter and believe that the country must confront systemic racism.

History hangs in the balance, unable to speak. Historical outcomes are far from clear and anything but inevitable; no one, however, should mistake peace for quiet, nor mistake the rage over police violence for indifference to the roots of *policy* violence and *poverty* violence. The ruthless indifference to the poor by our federal and state governments was clear well before COVID-19 laid it bare in 2020. Over half of American children come from poor or low-wealth families. According to the *American Journal of Public Health*, 250,000 Americans die of poverty each year. Cries of "I Can't Breathe" call out in compelling shorthand America's enduring racial chasm in every measure of well-being: health care and infant mortality, wages and wealth, unemployment, education, housing, policing and criminal justice, water quality and environmental safety. The hour of timid reforms has passed; the time for robust reconstruction seems to have come. But deep-seated and racially driven opposition is certain.

Though many newly aroused observers no doubt start this historic moment when the whole nation watched a Minneapolis police officer squeeze the life out of George Floyd by kneeling on his neck for eight or nine minutes, this began earlier. The beginnings and endings of things are always questionable, but this story definitely cannot begin with Ahmaud Arbery, though for millions of Americans, particularly those of a darker hue, the murder of Wanda Cooper-Jones's son seemed yet another marker of the age. The killing of unarmed African Americans by police officers or vigilantes claiming the authority of law enforcement, and often recorded by our seemingly ubiquitous cell phone video cameras, has become commonplace. *Black Lives Matter* is not just a slogan or a hashtag, but an actual organization, conceived and launched by Black queer women, which arose from protests after the killing of Trayvon Martin on February 26, 2012, and the subsequent acquittal of his security-guard killer the following summer. But the phrase quickly became shorthand for African American–led resistance to vigilante or police murder of unarmed Black people, although groups like the Dream Defenders, Black Youth Project 100, and the Movement for Black Lives, among countless others, also arose to combat these injustices. Like the term *Freedom Riders*, which in the early 1960s became a label for any civil rights activist, whether or not they had been on the buses, the words *Black Lives Matter* began to signify all Americans organizing to stop police violence or fight for racial justice.

Protesters chant "Say His Name!" and "Say Her Name!" and invoke long litanies of the victims—names like Oscar Grant III, Eric Garner, Tamir Rice, Michael Brown, Sandra Bland, Walter Scott, Philando Castile, Breonna Taylor, Ahmaud Arbery, and George Floyd, all of them killed in recent years, unarmed, at the hands of police officers. The insurgents of this "racial reckoning" do this to acknowledge the historical resonance of these killings, often invoking also the name of Emmett Till. These killings have become symbols of the destructiveness of white supremacy and many white Americans' ruthless indifference to or outright endorsement of anti-Black violence and injustice.

The dozens and dozens of wrongful incarcerations and death sentences of people of color—and often their exoneration after years in prison—also became an urgent issue. African Americans and their antiracist allies responded with demonstrations that raged from coast to coast and fueled scores of local campaigns. Although police brutality and the misuse of criminal justice systems provided the most urgent grievances, these cruelties became a national metaphor for our racial nightmares. They became symbols for a range of festering racial problems: chasms of inequality between Black and white and rich and poor; the criminalization of Black bodies; the militarization of police; mass incarceration and judicial injustice; that almost half of African American children grow up in a deindustrialized and impoverished urban wasteland; vast and enduring racial disparities in virtually every measure of well-being, from employment and unemployment to education and opportunity, housing and health care; and the location of toxic waste dumps in communities of color all over the country, particularly in the states of the former Confederacy. As a new spirit of protest and revolt arose, so did fervent hopes that perhaps the visual images of a murderous social order and the fervent uprisings of a new generation of freedom fighters might redeem and transform America. Though this nation remains ensnared in its long history of systemic violence and racial injustice, the struggle to end this nightmare is always evolving. Like racial injustice, these struggles are an enduring echo of the past, and deeply resonant among the human beings crammed into our jails and prisons. That echo, perhaps best embodied by the African Americans who constitute 13 percent of America's population but 42 percent of the occupants of death row, includes the voices of the Black men who tell their stories, affirm their humanity, and trace the prospects for our own in these pages.

Resources for Deeper Connection

As mentioned in "About the Stories," we offer this list of resources for those readers eager to engage in healing the harm and restoring—or perhaps initiating—kindness, compassion, and wholeness across our communities. These resources focus on transformation, both personal and systemic, because both are required if we are truly to envision new pathways toward healing. From their varied positions as scholars and lawyers and residents of death row, these women and men speak eloquently of a possible United States, one that has addressed its racist and classist history with insight and conscious action. As you read these titles, I hope one or two will engender that feeling of "Oh, this! This is what I need to hear."

Most fundamentally, these books remind us that what we have created, we can change. As a friend of mine often says, "It ain't that deep." In a very tangible way, she is right. The need is obvious. The time is now. So we do what needs to be done with courage, conviction, and gratitude for the opportunity to set right a mighty wrong.

Changing Lenses: A New Focus for Crime and Justice, by Howard Zehr
Dead Man Walking: An Eyewitness Account of the Death Penalty in the United States, by Sister Helen Prejean
The Death of Innocents: An Eyewitness Account of Wrongful Executions, by Sister Helen Prejean
Finding Freedom: Writings from Death Row, by Jarvis Jay Masters

Incarceration Nations: A Journey to Justice in Prisons around the World, by Baz
  Dreisinger
Just Mercy: A Story of Justice and Redemption, by Bryan Stevenson
Living without Enemies: Being Present in the Midst of Violence, by Samuel
  Wells and Marcia A. Owen
The Redemption Project with Van Jones (https://www.cnn.com/shows
  /redemption-project-van-jones)
The Sun Does Shine: How I Found Life and Freedom on Death Row, by
  Anthony Ray Hinton with Lara Love Hadin
Until We Reckon: Violence, Mass Incarceration, and a Road to Repair,
  by Danielle Sered